I0035511

TRAILBLAZERS WHO LEAD

Visionary Author Kearn Crockett Cherry
Foreword Author Gloria Mayfield Banks
Expert Author Dr. Cheryl Wood
Expert Author Theresa Royal Brown

Copyright © 2020 by Little Publishing LLC

All rights reserved. No portion of this book may be reproduced, stored in a retrieval system, or transmitted by any means electronic, mechanical, photocopy recording, scanning, or other except brief quotations without prior written permission of the publisher, except in case of brief quotations embodied in critical reviews and certain other non-commerical uses permitted by copyright law.

For permission requests, write to the publisher, addressed| "Attention Permissions Coordinator," at aalittle08@gmail.com

Book Cover Design: Little Publishing LLC

Published By: Little Publishing LLC

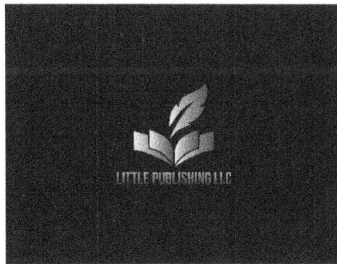

ISBN: 978-1-7343314-2-4

KEARN CROCKETT CHERRY

A Message From The Visionary Author

When you say Trailblazer many times the word "Fearless" follows it. Then you think of people like Oprah Winfrey, Bill Gates, Tyler Perry, Steve Jobs, John D. Rockefeller, Vanderbilt and so many others that are inspirational public figures. Rarely do you think of the individuals that assisted in building their empires because they work behind the scenes. These individuals are creating things that change the world, but they prefer not to be recognized. There are housewives who create organizations to feed the homeless. There are others who create organizations to give away scholarships. These individuals are just as determine and driven, but yet they are not as well known. I wanted to create a platform to allow individuals to share their story and how they are impacting the world in their own way. From the minister, attorney, doctor, and everyday people, all are passionate visionaries that are blazing the world! These powerful people never stop until their mission is complete.

I wanted to write about the stories of the "Unsung Trailblazers". When you look up the meaning of the word trailblazer, you will find risk taker, pioneer, visionary, relentless, collaborator, and pathfinder. Trailblazers follow their dreams, until it is done, with a relentless attitude.

I have been planning community events, programs and conferences for several years while working alongside some amazing women. Many of these powerful women create events and hire experts like myself to assist in making it a success. I have been able to observe these individuals who are never looking to be recognized, only to deliver something that the community needs. When you are creating things, you rarely think about who is watching. My new book anthology will help bring attention to the women who are quietly helping to shape the world with the things they are doing in their community. Hopefully, others will be inspired to share their stories while making their community a better place to live.

As a community leader, I realize that we create events and organizations in our community because we see there is a need for it. Many people are not willing to put in the time and money required to fill that need. Trailblazers do this because we are passionate and want to solve a problem, not because we want recognition. When I co-founded Success Women's Conference, the women on the Gulf Coast needed an event that would empower and recharge them. They were looking for ways to connect with women from around the nation. With a small leap of faith and a lot of determination, we were able to bring the conference into fruition. We have an average of over 1,000 attendees every year. I encourage you to stand up and be a trailblazer in your community. Trailblazers are a critical part of our society because they are reshaping our communities and taking the risks that other people are not willing to do. I hope you enjoy reading the stories shared in this book. Many of our authors are sharing their stories for the first time. Thank you for joining us on this journey. Happy Trails!

Your Visionary Author
Kearn Crockett Cherry
www.kearncherry.com

About Kearn Crockett Cherry

Kearn Cherry is the visionary author of "Trailblazers Who Lead". She is a motivational speaker, coach, entrepreneur and published author. She has been speaking for many years and is often referred to as the "Butts In the Seats Queen". She has a passion for networking and believes that networking increases your "net worth". As a collaborator, she has worked on various projects and events. She often presents on "Turning Connections into Profitable Collaborations".

Mrs. Cherry has been coaching for many years on "How to Create a Profitable Event" Live or Virtual. She has been in the healthcare industry for over 30 years and holds a degree in Occupational Therapy. She and her husband, Dennis Cherry are the owners of PRN Home Care which they have run for over 23 years old. They serve veterans, elderly and disabled patients in their home, nursing homes, hospitals and other facilities. They have three adult children, Dannan Cherry, business owner of Handy Dandy Moving, Dr. Jasmine Padgett, MD and Dr. Denise Cherry, DMD. She also has a grandson, Dannan Jr.

She is the co-founder and director of Success Women's Conference which has become a national conference with over 1,000 attendees yearly. She is the founder of the Power Up Summit as well. Mrs. Cherry has launched her new media network called KKonnections which will feature a radio, podcast and other digital platforms. She was the host and executive producer of her tv show, "Unwrinkled Heart Caregivers' Journeys". She co-founded and directed the R.I.P.E. Conference (Resources, Information, and Planning for the Elderly) and the Resources Guide for Caregivers.

Mrs. Cherry has been featured in numerous magazines including Essence Magazine as the "Comeback Queen" twice. She also has received many awards for her work in the community. In 2019, she was recognized by the Governor of Mississippi with the Governor's Initiative for Volunteer

Excellence (G.I.V.E.) Award for Outstanding Achievement in Empowerment Initiatives.

Contact: Kearn Crockett Cherry at www.kearncherry.com or kearn@prnhomecareservices.com.

TABLE OF CONTENTS

GLORIA MAYFIELD BANKS

Foreword

Gloria Mayfield Banks

A trailblazer is a person who sees a vision in front of her and decides to use it as courage to get there. She is not deterred or distracted by challenges, as the challenges are obstacles she uses to make her stronger. Using her wisdom she has acquired while building a new foundation of knowledge, she is a pioneer.

A trailblazer knows that there will be roadblocks, but it will not stop them from reaching the finish line. They create paths for others to navigate even if the journeys are different. She creates spaces for others and reaches back to make sure others benefit from the trail she provides.

My journey to success was a process. I was born and raised in a middle class household where my parents promoted self-esteem. As one of four girls, I attended Howard University and during my time there I worked at a grocery store where I learned business skills. Next, I attended Harvard University which was very challenging and got married where I endured ten years of domestic violence. Regardless of these circumstances, I always remained optimistic knowing that life is all about attitude and putting my goals at the forefront. While going through my divorce I was a single mother for seven years.

Entrepreneurship to me in many ways was absolute because I had no intention of becoming an entrepreneur. I was headed to the G-Suite but the glass ceiling went a different way for me in Corporate America. The journey took a turn for me to lead and educate professionals to achieve new levels of success. Out of 3.5 million women I became the First African-American in the company to rank #1 in North America and later #1 in the World. The most important thing I train on is building confidence and the most important skill I offer is emotional management.

Some of my challenges with building a team have been my optimistic attitude and bright light which have caused people to compare themselves to me which was very uncomfortable.

Despite having these powerful qualities, I had to overcome dimming my light for others. Becoming a single parent was a blessing and helped me tremendously in entrepreneurship. People who experience diversity go through confidence and financial issues. I was very passionate when I started my business and I believe people can get out get out of their own way in order to make powerful decisions that enable powerful outcomes. I'm obsessed with teaching people how to make a 100,000 a year. I'm obsessed with helping women make a lot of money that is not for material things, but the education they offer family members. Money makes a difference.

The biggest blessing for my career as a success strategist is the person I became in the process and the code I created in order to teach others. Kearn is a role model for women who mentor other women. When you see a woman who is passionate about supporting people's gifts, this is the greatest gift in business. To me that is the greatest legacy, working together to get to the top and understanding the need to propel others during your journey. You need other people in order to succeed. Many people don't have the passion to inspire others, offering them a springboard to success to gain even more. Kearn has accomplished that here.

About Gloria Mayfield Banks

Independent Elite Executive National Sales Director, International Speaker and Author

Dr. Gloria Mayfield Banks is an internationally renowned motivational success strategist and sales trainer, who has consistently beaten the odds to achieve extraordinary success. Dr. Banks holds a Bachelor's degree from Howard University, an MBA from Harvard University and an Honorary Doctorate from University of Maryland Eastern Shore. She has built a multi-million dollar enterprise, as an author, a founding partner of Charisma Factor, Inc. (a corporate event planning company), and as an Elite Executive National Sales Director with Mary Kay, Inc. In 2016 Gloria became the first African American in the history of the company to ranked #1 in North America. These accomplishments provided the foundation for her recently published book, Quantum Leaps, with ten specific steps to help you soar.

With her high energy and inspirational teaching style, Dr. Banks is best described as "Energy in Motion!" Dr. Banks has trained professionals on six continents to achieve new levels of success. She is expressly passionate about working with winners to actualize their full potential. Dr. Banks was a featured as one of the worlds top entrepreneurs at Grant Cardone's 10XGrowth business conference. In addition, Dr. Banks has shared the stage twice with Oprah Winfrey speaking on, Empowering Women and Girls for Leadership and at the N Street Village foundation fundraiser to help homeless women.

Dr. Banks shared her secrets of success with national media audiences, appearing on CNN with Soledad O'Brien, ABC-TV, and CNBC with Donny Deutsch on "The Big Idea"; and has been featured in Fortune, Black Enterprise, Glamour, and Ebony Magazines. Dr. Banks has received numerous awards and national recognition. Harvard Business School documented Gloria's success in a case study titled, "Gloria Hilliard Mayfield at Mary Kay Cosmetics." She resides in Baltimore, Maryland with her husband Ken Banks. They share four adult children.

DR. CHERYL WOOD

Going Out Into The Deep Water
Then Inviting Others To Join You!
Dr. Cheryl Wood

Just the word itself – Trailblazer – sends goosebumps up-and-down my arms. Whenever I hear that world I automatically know it's synonymous with someone who is tenacious, courageous and bold, someone who is a risk-taker and a go-getter. A trailblazer is a person who is willing to go out into the deep water before anybody else in order to test the waters, explore, and then signal to everybody else that it's not as scary as it looks.

My journey as a trailblazer started in 2009, the moment I made the definitive decision that I was no longer going to just exist in life, but that I was going to live my life to it's fullest and become an inspiration for others to do the same. Living life to it's fullest for me meant creating my own definition of success, living life on my own terms, and believing in myself enough to actually pursue my big dreams. It meant swimming out into the deep, scary parts of life that I was unfamiliar with in order to explore what was possible. At the time, I wasn't even sure I had the strength, stamina or endurance to swim out in the deep water. After all, just trying to stay afloat in the shallow waters of life can oftentimes be challenging enough. Nonetheless, the shallow waters still always felt much easier, safer, and more predictable than the deep water. So, that's where I stayed for years... stuck in what appeared to be easy, safe, and predictable.

You see, I had become so comfortable right where I was – sitting behind a desk in a 10x10 cubicle in a big office building in Washington, DC with a fancy title as an Executive Legal Secretary making $75k/year. Not bad for a brown girl who grew up in poverty, was the product of a single-parent household and didn't have a college degree, right? Well, at least that's what I had told myself for the 15 years that I played that role.

But, in 2009, I experienced a shift. I was now a married, mom of three and everything I thought success meant had changed. I was no longer content punching a time-clock on a job everyday, building somebody else's dream, coming and leaving when they told me to, having my children in someone else's care for 12-hours a day, and having my salary capped on the job because I didn't have enough letters behind my name. I wanted so much more for myself. I had a deep-rooted desire to find my life's purpose and to become a trailblazer for my children so they could witness me going out into the deep water and know that they could do the same in their own lives. Not to mention, I had a profound desire for freedom – time freedom, financial freedom, and creative freedom. I wanted to be the boss of my own life!

Granted, I didn't have a master blueprint of "how" this shift was going to happen, but I did have the tenacity to just get started. I was willing to face my fears, not have all the answers, and to fall down and make mistakes along the way. In 2009, while still working my full-time job I made the leap into entrepreneurship as my way to freedom. I launched my own custom line of mommy t-shirts that I would sell at weekend events, conferences, tradeshows, private exhibits, and flea markets. Let me assure you, nothing about it was glamorous! The process was grueling: I would pack 10-15 boxes of t-shirts in my car to transport to the event, unload and set-up my vendor table, greet and talk to the potential customers who did show up, get crushed when potential customers didn't purchase, pack my 10-15 boxes of t-shirts that I didn't sell back into my car to transport home, then arrive home only to tell my husband I had sold only 4-5 t-shirts after being gone for a full day. Needless to say, it was exhausting. After months of this same process, I had to pull on every ounce of my inner strength not to throw in the towel. I had to remember that this journey wasn't just about me… it was also about all the onlookers who were still in the shallow waters watching and waiting for me to become a strong swimmer in the deep water so I could invite them in. So, I stuck with it. I kept showing up even when I didn't immediately manifest the results I wanted. That's what Trailblazers do!

Low-and-behold, 18 months into the journey I got the phone call that shifted the trajectory of my life. I'll never forget answering the phone and hearing the person on the other end say, "Ms. Wood, I'm calling you from Morgan State University. We heard about your t-shirt business and we want to invite you to be one of our speakers at our annual women's conference. We want you to speak about how you got started in business and to share tips for other moms who want to start their own businesses." I burst out laughing and adamantly replied, "Clearly, you have dialed the wrong number." To this day, I still laugh whenever I recall that story because it reminds me of how unqualified I felt for such a long time. Even though I had been taking the risk of swimming in the deep water and making it look easy and seamless, it had been harder than anything I had ever done. It had tested my endurance, perseverance, discipline, and determination. But, as unqualified as I felt when I got that phone call, I knew that growth never happens when you choose to stay the same. Even though I didn't feel qualified for that opportunity, I felt called and magnetized to the opportunity. So, I gave myself permission to say YES! I showed up at Morgan State University for that women's conference on September 18, 2010 to deliver my very first speech in front of a room of strangers with my palms sweating and my heart pounding. I took a deep breath and gave the women the best version of the real, authentic me. And it was that day that I discovered I WAS BORN TO SPEAK!!

It hit me in that moment… I was actually swimming in the deep water and getting stronger by the minute. I was no longer hanging out with everybody else in the shallow waters where it felt safe. The deep water that I had previously viewed as so scary and uncomfortable was actually enlightening and fulfilling. And, once I experienced what it felt like, I wanted as many other women as possible to experience the same feeling. That was the day I knew without a shadow of a doubt that I was a Trailblazer because my journey was bigger than me, and it felt amazing! I found so much fulfillment in being a beacon of inspiration, belief, and possibility for others.

After that day, it became my life's work to impact the lives of women globally to remind them of the greatness they already possess, to help them face their fears and do it anyway, to inspire them to take risks that scare them but grow them, to help them walk away from their comfort zone, and to empower them to raise the bar on their own expectations of what's possible for their lives. The more opportunities I had to serve women, I began to focus on empowering women to own the power of their story and unleash the power of their voice! As a trailblazer, I understand all too well that, "Your story is ABOUT you but it ain't FOR you".

Today, nearly 11 years after my first speaking engagement, I feel blessed to still be in the business of trailblazing. I still consistently go out into the deep water first to test and explore, and then invite other women globally to join me. Everyday, I challenge myself to do what scares me the most because that's where I gain access to the best version of me which in turn impacts every woman I get to serve. So, whether it's writing my next best-selling book, hosting an international women's conference in Paris, France, traveling to South Africa to inspire and motivate college-aged girls, or speaking to leaders at NASA, I remain intentional about creating my "living legacy" on a daily basis without apologies or regrets! I've had the opportunity to serve thousands of women globally as a trailblazer hanging out in the deep water and bringing as many women with me as possible.

If you're that person who is still lingering in the shallow waters because it feels easy, safe, and predictable but you know you belong in the deep water, here is my Daily Call To Action so that you can experience the shift you've been desiring and also become a trailblazer:

1. Be intentional about making your faith stronger than your fears.

2. Upgrade your "internal dialogue" so the words you're speaking to yourself are in alignment with your big dreams.

3. Remove all toxic thinking, attitudes, behaviors, **and people** from your immediate environment.

4. Give yourself grace to make mistakes, learn from them, and still grow.

5. Abandon procrastination and any ideas of perfectionism at all costs.

6. Do not seek external validation or permission from anyone else to be the trailblazer you were born to be.

7. Find a community who will love and support you on the journey to who you're becoming.

8. Always remind yourself that You are enough! You are capable! You are worthy!

About Dr. Cheryl Wood

Dr. Cheryl Wood is an international empowerment speaker, 11x best-selling author, leadership expert, and master speaker development coach. She equips women leaders with the tools to own their story and unleash the power of their voice. Dr. Wood has trained countless women leaders across the United States and abroad in South Africa, India, France, United Kingdom, Canada and Bahamas. She empowers women to get out of their comfort zone, take calculated risks, and create a living legacy using their voice.

Dr. Wood has been featured on ABC, Radio One, Forbes Magazine, Huffington Post, ESSENCE, Black Enterprise, Good Morning Washington, Fox 5 News, Fox 45 News, The Washington Informer, The Baltimore Times, Afro-American Newspaper and numerous other media outlets. She has delivered keynote presentations organizations including NASA, FBI, U.S. Department of Defense, U.S. Department of Agriculture, The United Nations, National Association of Legal Professionals, Federally Employed Women, Blacks In Government, Verizon, PR News and the Congressional Black Caucus. (www.CherylEmpowers.com)

THERESA ROYAL BROWN

Trailblazing Out Of A Rock Bottom Experience
Theresa Royal Brown

The word "Trailblazer" is given to a person who blazes a trail for others to follow. This person is usually the "first" to do certain things that some would say won't work, but trailblazers do them anyway. People will sit back and watch to see if they succeed or fail before jumping out to try it themselves. A trailblazer takes risks and sometimes those risks work out, but many times they don't. In short, a true trailblazer has a big idea, concept or vision and they take a leap of faith to execute it. Many would argue that Michelle Obama is a trailblazer. Oprah is also another true trailblazer. Beyonce and Lizzo are most definitely trailblazers as well. Over the years I too have been called a "trailblazer" for the many ideas, concepts and events that I have introduced starting in 2006 until now. However, I haven't always felt like a trailblazer, in fact, many days I felt like a failure and wanted to give up. Somehow, someway, I have managed to stay the course no matter how bad things were. Why? Because that is what leaders and visionaries do, we pick ourselves up, dust ourselves off, and keep it moving. It hasn't been easy but I trailblazed myself out of my rock bottom experience, bounced back and learned valuable life lessons.

My trailblazer journey officially began on June 30, 2004, the day my mother dropped dead. At the time of her death she was an eight-year cancer survivor and was in excellent health. One minute she was fine, but the next minute she was gone. I realized on that date life was indeed very short and I needed to get moving with my event planning business that was sitting dormant. I decided to step out on faith and just get started.

I wish I could say that things have been easy and blazing my own trail has been all peaches and cream, unfortunately that has not been the case. Things started off well when I secured a three-year contract with a new client out of St. Louis, MO that was a referral. Over the years, I am pleased to say that I have done no advertising at all for my business and 95% of the business I get is referral-based. The other 5% has come from me directly reaching out to companies on LinkedIn that I would like to align with. That is also a trailblazer move to be brave enough to reach out to complete strangers, connect with them and have them become your client. I have been trailblazing for years and just didn't realize that is what I was doing.

Being an event planner, I was used to doing things on my own and never delegated or asked for help. That is not a good philosophy and I realized my unwillingness to ask for help or delegate caused me to be stagnant and I was unable to scale up my business. I finally learned this lesson later in my career, and I am glad I now understand that delegation is a sign of good leadership skills and asking for help shows strength, not weakness.

Along the way I did do some things incorrectly and I believe if I had done things the right way, I know I would have saved myself a lot of heartache. I won't bore you with the myriad of incorrect things I did, but I do want to provide you with a few correct things to keep you bouncing forward so you won't ever have to worry about bouncing back from a rock bottom experience. Practice the following:

1. Keep God first and pray before you accept any client.

2. Get a signed contract and deposit upfront, especially if the scope of work is massive.

3. Keep your business and personal life very separate.

4. If it doesn't feel right in your gut, don't do it.

5. Research and observe your potential client interaction on social media. Are they positive or negative?

6. Don't put all your eggs in one basket and make sure you have multiple clients.

Unfortunately, I didn't do some of the things I mentioned above and it hurt me in the long run. My first big client wasn't stable, they were unethical, had financial problems and eventually stopped paying my monthly retainer. This was my ONLY client, by choice because I wanted to give them personalized service, and not having other revenue streams sent my finances into a tailspin. I was unable to pay my mortgage and couldn't keep up with my other bills. I had always been a stickler about my credit and for most of my life, I had a perfect 850 credit score. All that changed because of the bad decision I made to take on this client when I had a bad gut feeling about them.

Due to my retainer being cut off and not having any other clients in the pipeline, I was forced to file bankruptcy to keep my home from going into foreclosure. For someone with a perfect credit score to have to file bankruptcy, it was a very traumatic experience. I lived alone and was broke... so broke that my car sat parked because I had so little gas that I was afraid if I drove anywhere, I wouldn't make it back home. Now that is broke! I was too proud to ask for help so I suffered for weeks before I finally broke down and filed for bankruptcy. The financial stress and pressure had taken a toll on me, and I felt like giving up.

Thoughts of suicide swirled in my head and I made the decision to end my life in February, 2007. That was my rock bottom moment. However, by the grace of God, a friend called me at the right moment and talked me off the ledge. She encouraged me, ministered to my spirit and that one conversation got me back on track. I thank God that He sent someone to help me when I refused to reach out on my own.

The most important realization I received from the conversation I had with my friend was that my filing bankruptcy wasn't the end of the world and I would get through that bumpy period. That was the beginning of my bounce back. It became clear to me that I believed my credit defined me and when I lost it, I felt a part of me was gone. Credit is important, but not enough to idolize or end your life over. I also realized that God would provide for me regardless of my credit situation, I just needed to depend on Him. I am pleased to say that I have been depending on Him from that day to this one.

Over the years I decided that I wanted to do something to give back to other entrepreneurs who might be struggling to get business. I decided to form a networking organization, Entrepreneurs and Professionals Network (EPNET), which is a business building organization for entrepreneurs and leaders. For nearly 15 years, this organization has been my community give back where I host networking sessions and workshops to connect entrepreneurs together to build relationships and deeper connections. EPNET has connected thousands of entrepreneurs over the years in the DC, MD and VA area, and has generated million dollar deals within our network. I also started the EPNET Legacy Awards, the first in the DMV area, which honored entrepreneurs each year leaving a living legacy. In addition, I also started an entrepreneur camp for children to teach them the in's and out's of entrepreneurship. At the end of the camp scholarships are given to the 3 top students who present the best business plan, and seed money is given to them to help start and/or grow their business.

I also wrote my first book in 2009 and then re-released it as a second edition in 2012. Since then I have written 2 other books and was in 2 book collaborations. I have ventured out into the publishing world and have helped 6 authors write and publish their own books as well. I also have several other books of my own that will be released in the near future.

Bouncing back from setbacks takes time, it takes tenacity and it takes an iron will to keep going. I often wonder how many lives would have been affected if I didn't keep fighting and didn't keep blazing my own trail to help others. I am glad I didn't quit.

Being a trailblazer means to NEVER give up, NEVER give in to self-doubt and NEVER listen to the haters. In spite of my rock bottom experience, I thank God that I was able to keep moving, changed my focus, and kept on blazing my own trail.

About Theresa Royal Brown
Event Producer Extraordinaire & Master Networker

Theresa is the Chief Event Producer at Premiere Events Management and Master Networker at Entrepreneurs and Professionals Network (EPNET). In some circles she is known as the "Master Networker" because she has the ability to connect like-minded people together to build solid business relationships. She encourages team building through networking events and workshops. In other circles she is known as the "Event Producer Extraordinaire" because she has a "gift" of creating one of a kind, unique and memorable experiences. In addition, she is the author of several books: "Not Built To Break - Becoming Resilient Through Life Challenges", "Wisdom - Words To Inspire You To Create Your Legacy", and most recently, two mini-books entitled "Top Level Connections - Tips To Become A Master Networker" and "The Student Action Guide To Building Relationships." She is married to her partner in life and business, and the man she adores, Charles L. Brown, Jr.

DR. JENNIFER SUTTON

Winds of Transformation

Dr. Jennifer Sutton

I can still close my eyes and vividly experience the feelings, sights, sounds and smells from that day. It was August 30, 2005, and in an instant my house had been completely destroyed - reduced to a clean, concrete slab. I was 7 month's pregnant with twin girls and held firmly to the hand of my two-year-old son as the scene unfolded. It was a terrifying, confusing, emotional time. As I reflect today, I am grateful for the winds of Hurricane Katrina that have transformed me into the servant leader that I am today.

Prior to that moment, my husband and I were veterinarians and owners of a veterinary hospital we had opened just two years prior. Thankfully, it was spared from destruction. Before that day, I lived an insulated, comfortable life of work, home and building our family. Although I was a boss, I was not a *leader*. The immediate days following Hurricane Katrina were a blur. I am still overcome with emotion as I reflect upon the outpouring of support during the aftermath. I remain in awe that so many would give so much time, talent and treasure to complete strangers without expectation of reward, repayment or recognition. It's this experience that sparked my desire to "pay it forward" as I began my personal transformation into *servant leadership*.

Following the safe and healthy arrival of my twins and our relocation to a new home, I began volunteering as a court-appointed special advocate (CASA). The CASA program trains community volunteers to advocate for the desires of children in foster care, essentially serving as their "voice" within the court system. Additionally, I became the trainer and handler of a search and rescue dog after watching their work following Hurricane Katrina. Both these volunteer opportunities provided tremendous satisfaction and increased my awareness of the pressing needs in my surrounding community. My volunteerism truly "filled my cup" in ways that traditional paid work could not. Through my service to others, in many respects I received more than I gave. It also taught me fundamentals of *servant leadership* such as empathy, stewardship, and the desire to build and support my surrounding community.

In 2013, I was offered the opportunity to serve as interim executive director of our local CASA program. It was an honor to be considered, but also a large commitment because it required me to step away from my veterinary practice for a time. This experience provided considerable opportunity to become intimately aware of community challenges and needs, and significantly impacted my leadership transformation. Working with volunteers and fundraising was incredibly humbling and rewarding work. Unlike previous roles of managing and dictating tasks to employees, I quickly realized if I assumed the role of a servant and supported volunteers I was much more effective. Showing gratitude and appreciation and offering myself as a servant to their needs inspired and motivated them and the program flourished. Looking through the eyes of our "clients", children in foster care, and encouraging volunteers to meet their needs as servants, improved case outcomes to ultimately reunite children with their families.

My husband, supportive but growing tired of my long hours as the CASA director, asked I rejoin our practice. We were preparing to move into a new facility and it was increasingly demanding to balance the needs of our practice using our current management structure and our family of four children under the age of ten. Stepping back into my practice, I intentionally instituted the same techniques I found successful in my CASA position. Additionally, I focused on the culture and people of our organization, not just the product.

Taking a critical look at our services through our clients' perspective was enlightening. We asked questions such as: Are we effectively meeting their needs? What are their problems and how can I work to solve them? How can I enrich the lives of their pets? Answers provided insight into opportunities. I also evaluated our culture, asking: Are my employees genuinely happy? Are they actively engaged? Do they really understand and demonstrate our values and vision? Uncomfortably, I realized the answer to many of these questions was a resounding "no". It was personally challenging to undergo this internal assessment but it gave me direction as

I transformed the way I lead my team and began to become their servant leader.

Looking from my clients' perspective, I identified several services I could implement and improve to better *serve* them. For example, we expanded our hours so we could be available for clients during times when their traditional veterinarian was not. We also improved delivery of care through environmental and physical changes, and training minimized stress clients experienced. Alternate payment methods were also instituted for large, unexpected expenses and our customer service experience was evaluated and enhanced.

Employee development was a critical component of my transformation. All employees interviewed to ensure current duties matched personal interests. Job satisfaction was discussed, as well as ways where they felt they could be better supported or served. When asking their "why"- *why* they chose to work within my business when there were other available opportunities - interestingly, salary, benefits, and schedules were rarely their answers. Typically, reasons were cultural-driven, and vision- and mission–oriented, such as our community reputation, service mentality, and that they felt value and support as part of our team. As interests emerged, team members were "championed" to make special projects or areas their own. Resoundingly, performance as individuals and as a team excelled; personal and professional goal setting was celebrated; applicable education and career paths - even if, ultimately, they did not remain in my employ - were encouraged; employee benefits were overhauled; and regular team meetings were encouraged to open communication. The more focused I became on individual employee success, treating them as fully capable and resourceful individuals, the more their performance excelled. Individuals settled into productive places within our team. For some, it even meant realizing they desired something outside our organization and felt compelled to change career or employment paths. In hindsight, most of these individuals were disengaged and actually had subpar performance. Coming to their own realization that they desired a change was powerful and prevented the negative impacts created by intentionally removing team members.

I continued to develop *myself*. I read books, sought and completed advanced business courses, participated in leadership development, and collaborated with mentors and peers, enabling me to recharge my passion for my profession and my team. As I grew so did my employees. Awareness of emotional intelligence, personality traits, and communication styles greatly impacted the way I lead and has been instrumental in my transformation.

The more I continued my personal evolution, community engagement and employee development, the more servant leadership began to reflect my leadership style. I moved from a managerial role to a motivator. Business culture shifted from one that focused on present actions and profits to one that, through the lens of customer service, provided value. Culture and service were refined and evolved to a point where it couldn't be easily duplicated by competitors.

While personal and professional accolades have not been the inspiration for my leadership evolution, the result of my servant leadership transformation is reflected in significant business growth and success. Our business, Gulf Coast Veterinary Emergency Hospital, was included in the 2017 Inc. 5000 list as one of the fastest growing, privately-owned businesses in America. In 2019, my husband and I were named the Small Business Association Business Persons of the Year for the state of Mississippi. Personal community engagement has led to numerous local accolades I'm proud of. Today, I remain involved in several community organizations in a variety of supportive roles that still fulfill me more than paid work can.

Business culture development has truly been my "secret sauce". A supportive environment developed from the "bottom up" as a servant led to increased employee engagement, satisfaction, and productivity. It is positive culture, employee satisfaction, engagement, and loyalty to our team that has been the mainstay of continued success.

I quote John Maxwell, "If you want to become the best leader you can possibly be, no matter how much or how little natural leadership talent you possess, you need to become a serving leader". Start locally by serving others, just as I did when I felt compelled to "pay it forward" after one of the most challenging experiences of my life. Enjoy the personal satisfaction that service to others provides. Continue your personal and professional growth and realize your "why". Apply the same principles and heart to your organization. Start from the bottom, with those that are struggling the most, and as you empower them, move upward. A successful team will slowly unfold and evolve to reveal itself like a butterfly leaving a cocoon. A supportive and positive culture infuses new life and motivation into your team.

Had it not been for the winds of Hurricane Katrina, I probably wouldn't have embarked on my *transformation* into servant leadership. It's not finished and continues today as I develop my skills to teach others how to create their own positive and productive cultures. I am thankful for the gift those winds provided me. I hope, without being motivated by tragedy, you embark on your own transformative journey to become the servant leader you're meant to be!

About Dr. Jennifer Sutton

Jennifer Sutton, DVM, MBA is a wife, mother, veterinarian and successful entrepreneur. In the face of personal tragedy; she felt compelled to a life of volunteer service primarily as an advocate for marginalized people and animal populations. Her experiences have been motivational, rewarding and fulfilling in ways that her traditional career was not.

As a volunteer servant to others, she applied these same principles within her businesses and transformed into a servant leader. The results have been extraordinary. Through implementation of servant leader ideals like empathy, compassion, awareness and stewardship; she has created a generative and successful culture. Among her accomplishments are numerous community accolades, inclusion in the Inc. 5000 business list and being named the Mississippi Small Business Association's Businessperson of the Year. She is currently developing her skills and knowledge to be able to assist others in becoming the servant leaders that they were meant to be!

CONSTANCE WOULARD

Humility In Leadership

Constance Woulard

As a trailblazer for leadership, I have been afforded perspectives that provide a plethora of experiences in which to build and develop our leadership style. The prevalence of leadership theories and practical experiences provide an opportunity to assess and enquire about issues and concepts, which allow an opportunity to problem-solve, lead and guide on a daily basis.

Each of us are leaders, whether at home, in work leadership positions, or in our community - we have all been called to lead. Leadership is a life journey guiding others through daily life processes. It is a commitment and a responsibility to those we lead, not for the self.

I framed this chapter on humility as I believe it is the foundation of leadership. For me and not by choice, humility began at seven years old, by giving up freedom to play with friends after school due to commitments to the family's electronic business. My leadership journey began to evolve at that very moment, beyond my recognition. This was the beginning of my leadership skills development.

Selflessly, at that time I looked forward to being present and productive in my workplace. It was there I learned customer service and giving respect and service to others. I embarked upon this leadership journey years before I was aware of what was occurring.

Humility is an important leadership trait. It is an effective tool for leading and motivating others, as well as stimulating productivity in a variety of leadership arenas. Humility, in its broadest sense, instills self-awareness, the appreciation of other people's strengths, of being receptive to new ideas, and insight into personal self-performance. True humility requires courage and trust that stem from a leader's self-confidence and capabilities. Humility may be viewed as a weakness in leadership, however, on the contrary, it is a true strength of leadership. Great leaders know who they are; they know what they want; and they believe in their ability to achieve their goals. At the same time, great leaders understand they cannot achieve their goals on their own. Leaders should rely upon others to accomplish goals and tasks. They should coexist and function collaboratively. It is important for leaders to recognize they are not required to have all the answers. Leaders must establish credibility, as well as provide tools and metrics for managing uncertainty.

In leadership, is easy to become attracted to self-gain and status. Leaders who exercise humility are often viewed as effective and they are able to establish credibility in the face of humility in leadership. Trust is established and opportunities for learning exists for all stakeholders. Those who lead from a perspective of humility utilize their own personal successes for the good of the team or organization. To lead with humility promotes an environment of success, as well as the edification of others, which is the leader's main focus.

Over the years I have learned so many lessons as I have blazed the trail of leadership. I arrived at the realization that as a true leader, I must remove the self from the equation at all times. It is important to be cognizant of the needs of people so I can them effectively - ego has no place in leadership. Humility requires leaders to remain objective in decision-making. It is important for leaders to have authenticity and integrity. Those we lead must be able to trust us as individuals, as well as trust our guidance and decision-making. Humility must remain a priority of leadership.

As a leader, I have evolved from a more authoritarian approach to a style of leadership which embraces authenticity and humility. Through trial and error and a vast amount of life and leadership experiences, my leadership style is one of competence, courage, and respect.

Regardless of where I am along this leadership journey, it is necessary for me as a leader to focus on the legacy I choose to leave for those who are currently trailblazing with me, and for those who follow. I must then decide my leadership's future direction, and what I wish to achieve and accomplish as I develop others.

About Constance Woulard

Constance Woulard is a native of Gulfport, Mississippi. In her current role as Divisional Director of Nursing and Utilization Management, she is accountable for nursing practice and quality across her organization, encompassing twelve sites within the United States. Ms. Woulard has served as a faculty adjunct with Grand Canyon University and the University of Phoenix. She is currently a teaching associate with the University of North Carolina at Wilmington. Her proudest accomplishments are as follows:

- Mother of one son
- Dual Master's prepared nursing leader
- Motivational speaker and nursing educator
- Long-term care consultant
- Dedicated to developing the next generation of leaders
- Founder and owner of AWG Consulting
- Founder and owner of Connie Cakes Unlimited
- Established cooking site---Cooking with Style by Constance

DAWN LIECK

Doing it Scared
Dawn Lieck

I learned at a very young age that fear could totally debilitate me. I would fear doing things that were out of my comfort zone, but also fear not doing those very same things. This rendered me frozen, stuck and unfulfilled. I was mad at myself for being to afraid to even try. I remember once at work I had started a new position that required me to speak in front of my coworkers in a meeting - about 100 people attended. On the Friday my promotion was announced, my supervisor said "Dawn will share some upcoming events with you. Dawn, please come on up." The fear hit me so hard I immediately ran from the meeting to the restroom and threw up. It was sheer terror.

Why did I react with such fear? These were all my friends. What was I so afraid of? What could have possibly happened that could justify my fear? What worst case scenario would happen if I spoke in front of that audience? Would I die? Of course not! After that day (I call it "THE INCIDENT") I really had to do some soul searching to figure out why I let irrational fears control so many aspects of my life. I wasn't reaching my potential in my career. I wasn't happy with my personal life. I lived in fear of anything new or different. I was such a creature of habit that even rearranging my furniture would trigger anxiety. Things just had to change! My life was passing me by as I stood frozen in fear.

Then I had an epiphany! As I contemplated doing something new, the fear crept in.

I asked myself why? Answer: Because you can't!

I asked myself why? Answer: Because it's too hard!

I asked myself why? Answer: I don't know how!

31

I asked myself why? Answer: I haven't even tried to learn how!

You get the point. I did this every time fear tried to prevent me from making a move. I asked myself over and over until I hit the real *why*. The actual reason was that I was holding myself back. You have to be honest with yourself. I called this the "Why Method". The more times I asked myself "why" the closer I came to the root cause of my fear. It never had anything to do with the initial fear preventing me from taking action on my goals. Nine times out of ten, the bottom line was fear of failure. Once you get to the bottom of the actual issue and face it head on, fear will no longer have a hold on you. Fear, in the face of rational thought, loses its power.

When you have a goal, face your fear! So what if you fail? You won't die, I promise! Different outcomes require different actions. If you fail, try again! Make a new plan. Adjust your goal. Maybe start small and work your way up. The only reason anyone fails is if they don't try.

I knew my life was not at all what I wanted it to be and it would never change unless I changed it. I went full speed ahead and did it scared - more terrified, if I am being truly honest. I continued to use my "Why" method every time negative self-talk and fear reared its ugly head. By facing my fears head-on and pushing myself to succeed, my life began to change - drastically! I left a job and a marriage, both I spent over 20 years in! Talk about turning my life upside down. This was lightyears beyond rearranging furniture! Granted I didn't die, however, some days I was sure I would. Change is no small undertaking, especially for someone who had let fear control most of her adult life. Transforming my life was the hardest thing I've ever done.

To transform my life, I had to fight myself, for myself, every single day. It was the battle of a lifetime. When things became uncomfortable, I wanted to run back to my old life, my comfort zone. I had to resist the urge to backtrack every single day. Well, let me tell you sister, I owned that struggle. I persevered and I was triumphant! Through it all I had to stay true to myself, to be the person who lived without fear, the person who would be brave enough to succeed.

I can't tell you how astounding it is to look back at the old me. In my life before I had made the conscious decision to change everything. My old life is now just a distant memory. No more wasted time, missed opportunities or being frozen. It's been eleven years since I took my life back and divorced fear, with no alimony! Well, just like an ex-husband, fear doesn't go away easy. To this day, I still hear that voice in my head saying "You can't", "You're not good enough", "You can't succeed". Some days people might see me as too much - those are the days I've put on my warrior armor to combat the enemy. Fear! Remember that fear is never permanently defeated. No matter who you are the battle with fear is never over. You do what it takes to beat fear today and when you get up tomorrow be ready to Blaze That Trail again.

In my triumph over fear I have become the person I only dreamed I could be. I unapologetically put myself first. I understand in order to be completely free it has to be all about me. I have created a life I couldn't imagine was possible. I have become a transformation coach. I accompany women through their journey of change at any age. It's never too late! I'm also an international motivational speaker (no more throwing up!). And guess what? I do it scared every day. It makes every win so much sweeter. If it was easy, it wouldn't be nearly as fun!

Now I will say it has definitely not been an easy journey. Transformation is constant - I evolve every time I say *yes* to me and *no* to fear. Life is decisions and you make them every day. Who are you going to be? Will you be the person ruled by your fears or will you be the trailblazer you know you can be? Will you stay on the sidelines or are you ready to get in the game and win? When you make the decision to do it scared and be better tomorrow than you are today, you too can be finally *free*!

About Dawn Lieck

Dawn Lieck is a bold, out of the box, Transformation Coach. She is an International Motivational Speaker, Author and CEO of Finally Free LLC. Dawn is transforming lives of tenacious women who desire to thrive in self discovery and development. She is intentional about impacting women's lifestyles by providing them the tools to pursue their innermost dreams.

Dawn dives deep through sharing her authentic story of breakthrough and transformation. She has hosted incredible empowerment events and has spoken at numerous conferences with a powerful message of success and change. Dawn has coached public speakers from first time speakers to the advanced. Dawn is a board member of many business and charitable organizations including Lighthouse Business and Professional Women, Gulfport Chamber of Commerce, and Success Women's Conference to name a few.

Dawn is unstoppable and effective at transforming lives one day at a time!

You can reach Dawn at:

Finallyfree1llc@Gmail.com

https://www.facebook.com/FinallyFreeLLC/

DR. TOY L. WATTS

Change The Narrative
Dr. Toy L. Watts

There's no person in the world I wanted to make proud more than my grandmother. Josie was a confident, tell-it-like–it-is - even if it hurt your feelings - kind of person. Mama, as I called her, spent a lot of time trying to shape me into the person she thought I should become. To her, being a nurse was the most prestigious career for which I could ever qualify, and she worked hard on grooming me. "Toy! Bring that Vaseline and come put some on my feet." I'd sit on the ottoman and prop mama's foot on my knee and rub it and then she'd start her usual spill. "You know, you would make a great nurse. You do such a good job on my feet, and nurses make *good* money." When it was time for me to go to college, all I knew was I didn't want to be a nurse but I had better choose a career that brought in a lot of money, because that would be the only way I would win her respect.

It was the end of the first semester and I had to declare a major. After some soul-searching and reading the Dillard University catalog from cover to cover, I had made up my mind. I called Mama to tell her. "Mama, I've figured out what I want to do!" I could hear the excitement in her voice. She was ready for the big announcement. "What…?" she asked curiously. I was on the other line grinning from ear to ear. "I've decided I'm going to be a teacher!" After the words left my mouth I felt like the guy at the end of a tap dance routine when he stomps his foot and puts his hand out. Then mama let out the loudest smack I ever heard, "Girl! You gon' be in school for the rest of your life!" And then she handed the phone to my grandpa. "Hey Daddy, I've decided I'm going to be a teacher." He said, "Well, at least you'll always be employed." That certainly didn't go how I imagined. It was a turning point though. It was the moment I decided to LEAD my own life.

I started teaching the week of my 22nd birthday. I was teaching middle schoolers who were as tall as me, so I followed the old rule of thumb of not smiling at my kids until Christmas. I loved my job and especially my students, however, something on the inside kept telling me I was going to

do more, but I didn't know what that meant. So, I did a little of everything…
I coached, I tutored, I started a dance team, and I was in charge of the
science fair. My first principal was a hustler. He did all kinds of things to
make money for student incentives. Dances were the biggest money maker.
His hustle meant single rookie teachers like me would be volunteering at
dances on several Friday nights. I can still see him chaperoning the dance
looking like Superman with his hands on his hips as he surveyed the
happenings of the middle school dance scene. I remember looking at him
handing out nachos from the concession stand and saying to myself, "I
AIN'T ever gonna be a principal."

Leadership was calling me, but I didn't answer - I got a degree in school
counseling instead. After one year in that role, we moved and I went back
to teaching. A few months later, mama died. Since we were in a new place
I wanted to "just" teach and leave all the extra stuff I had normally done
behind. My principals in Atlanta decided differently. I was a team LEAD at
one school and I LEAD the implementation of departmentalized learning in
4th grade at another school. As Matthew 5:14 states, "A city that is set on a
hill cannot be hidden." My gifts made room for me. I could no longer deny
my true calling - leadership.

My daughter, Josie, named after mama, was 18 months old when I
completed my Ph.D. I had been the principal of an alternative school for
three years. I turned that school into a top-notch educational program for
my students. All my teachers were certified and were very committed to our
school. In my three years as principal, there wasn't a single fight and
students begged to stay with me at the alternative school. When I called my
superintendent to tell her I defended my dissertation, she was in shock. She
said, "Tell me what a determined person won't do!" I said, "Why are you
so surprised? I told you I was in school." She responded, "Everybody is in
school." Three months later, she came over and told me she was moving me
to another school. I took over an elementary school at a critical time in our
state. We changed accountability models, we moved to common core
standards, and we introduced the third grade gate that required third graders
to pass a reading test for promotion to the next grade level. In a difficult
time, my team and I moved mountains. We became a well-oiled machine.

We created a welcoming, safe environment with hard-working teachers and supportive parents, however, as soon as I was getting comfortable in my new position, God moved.

My husband was attending a community service event and ran into the new superintendent of the Moss Point School District. After she learned I was his wife, she told him she had heard great things about my work. After that chance conversation with my husband, I sat in front of the new superintendent for Moss Point to interview for a job. She and I clicked and she hired me to be her assistant superintendent. We worked nonstop. I had an 18-month-old and a four-year-old, and I commuted more than an hour one way to work. We were making significant changes in the district. The high school received its first B rating in the history of the state's accountability model, the graduation rate improved, we had the most significant growth numbers for pre-kindergarten on the coast, and we were making steady progress on the accountability model overall. I had baby number three and I was settled and comfortable to continue the work.

One morning in September, I got an email announcement for a superintendent vacancy in Laurel. It hit me in my gut. I knew this was my moment. Immediately, doubt set in. "Why now? I'm not ready. I need a little more time. I'm not going to apply. I need to work on my resume." Then I opened the application. Two questions made it worse: What works have you published? What awards have you received? I said to myself, "See, I knew I wasn't ready. I haven't published anything. I mean, when would I have time for that? I have three small kids! Awards? I don't think certificates from church count." Then all of a sudden, I stopped the negative talk. In my mind I said, "I'm gonna apply anyway!"

I prayed. I went to my praying friends and asked for prayer. I specifically asked to just get into the room. I said, "God, my resume won't tell them who I really am. Get me in the room and they will know I am supposed to be the person to lead this district." I completed my application and sent it in. I researched the town, found my house, looked for activities, and watched the Internet daily for updates. I asked a friend to help me rehearse possible questions. I was ready. I kept thinking, any day now they will contact me for my interview. That weekend, my family and I went shopping for a suit. My husband believed in my conviction so much he bought me a purse to go with my new suit. The superintendent candidate interviews were going to be open to the community, so everything had to be just right.

The week following I heard nothing. I checked their website every day and there were no updates. That Friday night I checked again and they had posted the list of interviewees! I took a deep breath and went down every name on the list. Mine was not there. That was it. I wasn't going to get into the room. It wasn't my job after all.

Almost a month went by. Although I had made peace with the situation, I still checked the site every day. I wanted to know who got the job. Nothing had been announced. While in a meeting at work, I got a call from a strange number. I assumed it was my turn down call, but I was wrong. The school board had decided they wanted to interview a few more candidates. Prayers had worked and I was going to get into the room. Wearing my new suit, carrying my new purse, and exhibiting confidence learned from Mama Josie, I stood before the school board and a crowd of onlookers and I shared my vision, my passion, and the heart of Toy L. Watts.

The rest is history, literally. In 2018, I became the first female superintendent in the Laurel School District's 129 year history! I got into the room and they chose me as their leader. "Mama, I did alright... and I finished school, too!"

About Dr. Toy L. Watts

Dr. Toy L. Watts made history when she was named Superintendent of the Laurel School District in 2018. She is the first woman to serve as superintendent of education in the district's 129 years of educating the children of Laurel.

Dr. Watts received a Bachelor of Arts in Elementary Education from Dillard University, a Master of Education in School Counseling, a Specialist in Education in Educational Administration and a Doctor of Philosophy in Educational Administration from the University of Southern Mississippi.

Dr. Watts is a seasoned leader with over 22 years of experience in education, having served as a teacher, counselor, coach, principal, assistant superintendent and superintendent.

DR. AIMEE CLUTE

Faith That Works

Dr. Aimee Clute

My story is not a poor, pitiful me kind of story, but I believe it's one of courage and faith.

I was a P.K. (preacher's kid) and I was just twenty-one years old when I said "I do". I had no clue of what lay ahead for me, but I was in love and had just married the man of my dreams. Our plan was to evangelize the world. My faith had been tested and tried plenty of times. All my life I had been a part of ministry, which is certainly one of ups and downs, but I was up for the challenge. Now I would share a life of ministry with my husband.

Soon, we would welcome our first baby boy. It was a hard pregnancy and our baby came pre-maturely, causing him to have under-developed lungs. One day my husband, Thomas, placed a small cassette recorder playing Bible verses in the small NIC unit crib. We listened as the words that came forth from those tiny little speakers changed the atmosphere that surrounded our son and brought life into him, completely turning his life around. We were able to bring him home after staying in the NIC unit for only one week.

Shortly after, my husband accepted a pastoral position in Gulfport, MS. This was a whole new step for me. I had only evangelized, never pastoring or even staying in one place for any length of time over a few weeks. I went from meeting new people all the time to seeing the same faces week after week. It was a huge learning curve for me trying to develop relationships and realizing there was a gap between learning something unique about an individual and getting to know someone on a more personal level. It was also during this time I realized church people could actually be cruel and judgmental. I was never pretty enough or skinny enough; I couldn't play the piano or be the best mom possible. There was always something that seemed to prove how I just wasn't ever good enough.

While dealing with my own identity issues, my husband would soon be diagnosed with cancer and was told he only had three months to live. It wasn't something I ever expected to hear. By this time, our second child had arrived. I was twenty-five years old, and had no family to call upon locally. Many of our fellow ministers called to offer help with funeral services when the time came, but none of them offered to pray. I had never felt more alone.

I found myself having to fill in for my husband at times, while still leading worship. I felt I had to be the strong one. My mind set was, "The congregation can never see me cry." I thought if they saw me cry they would think I had given up hope and it would affect their faith, ultimately causing them to leave the church. This experience made me to realize that though I had a strong foundation of faith, I had to dig deeper. I knew I had to speak life to my husband or he was going to die, and I refused for death to be an option.

I started to not only just read the Word of God, but to study it in depth. Every day I sang to my husband and quoted the healing scriptures over him. After several months of doing these things continuously and my husband eating a healthy diet, the doctor gave him a clean bill of health. It had been quite the test, but once again faith pulled us through.

After all this took place, I began to deal with my own issues one by one. The test then became really personal. I found myself often crying when I looked in the mirror. Stress had made me put weight on and I now suffered from extreme psoriasis that covered my arms, ears, face and head that even led to severe hair loss. I felt ugly. I fought the hardest with these perceptions of myself, almost always before a church service knowing I had to minister to the people, but wondering how they viewed me as their leader. One day, after throwing a tantrum, my husband put me in front of the mirror and asked me these words: "What if someone's soul is at stake, today? Are you going to let what you see in the mirror keep you from ministering to that soul?" *Why did he have to bring God into this conversation?,* I thought to myself. I had always had a heart after God so how could I possibly let Him down? Those two questions broke me, but it was at this point God started

44

to put me back together. In my act of obedience, he started to restore my own body little by little. Oh, but that was only half my test.

I had sang gospel music since I was four years old. I performed at camp meetings and conventions, ranging from small congregations to thousands. By the age of eighteen, I had recorded numerous albums. However, at that time, I had been diagnosed with throat nodules, leaving me completely without a voice. A person couldn't have stabbed me in the chest and hurt me worse than that. Singing was my heart, my way of worship - It was how I communicated with God. Three months passed by, and still no voice. I could barely speak. It was then God began to deal with me about preaching. God knew I would argue with him on this one; so for me to listen he had to shut my mouth. In my mind, I rehearsed why I shouldn't answer the call, as if he didn't know what he was doing. But when I finally made my mind up to submit to his way, my voice returned full throttle. It was even better and stronger than what it was before I had lost it.

These were just a few of my beginnings. I am now fifty years old. My husband and I have both experienced the healing power of God in numerous ways over the years. Nonetheless, every day is a faith walk. If I hadn't learned to overcome fear, doubt, insecurities, and inadequacies, I would've never made it to who I am today.

I'm reminded of the song, "The Man in the Mirror". It had to start with me. Not only believing in myself, but knowing words like: I can do all things through Christ who strengthens me (Phil 4:13), or Being confident of this very thing, that he which hath begun a good work in you will perform it until the day of Jesus Christ (Phil. 1:6). And because I stand on His word, I've now had opportunities to minister all over the world.

My husband has faced cancer fourteen times now. He inspires me in this faith walk. I've learned there will be good days and bad days; times where there won't be a preacher, organ player or choir around. Sometimes, it's just me and God and His word to get me through.

In Hebrews 11:1, it states, "Now faith is the substance of things hoped for, the evidence of things not seen."

In Ephesians 3:20, it says, "Now to him who is able to do exceedingly abundantly above all that we ask or think, according to the power that works in us."

What is that power? It is the Will to believe and it encourages me to live life at its fullest each and every day, taking nothing for granted.

To the single mother struggling to meet bills and feed her children; to the widow who feels alone or abandoned; to the one who has been diagnosed with a terminal disease; to the one who is dealing with the loss of a child; to the one who is struggling with self-esteem; to the one who is looking for acceptance; to the one who has been hurt by a failed marriage or relationship; to the one who hates what she sees when she looks in the mirror; to the one fighting depression; to the one who feels rejected or was abused; to the one dealing with substance abuse - may your will to believe not only be the power source you need to pull you through, but to be an overcomer in the end.

The biggest obstacle we have to overcome is our self and our mind set, thought processes, and perceptions. Whatever we allow ourselves to Believe is what we allow God to do for us in our lives. I encourage each individual who reads this to find the scripture that speaks to you in your situation and hold on to it. That scripture is your evidence and confidence that God is for you, with you, and will never leave you.

About Dr. Aimee Clute

Dr. Aimee Clute celebrates forty years of full time ministry, holding a doctorate in Divinity and a certificate of Chaplaincy. Dr. Aimee is celebrating twenty-nine years of marriage to Apostle Thomas Clute having two sons, one daughter, and two grandchildren. Apostle and Dr. Clute have pastored the "River of Life Church" in Gulfport, Mississippi for twenty-eight years.

Dr. Aimee has appeared on television broadcasts and has had the privilege of ministering in grand arenas before persons of great political influence, as well as, alongside prominent ministers and artists. Dr. Clute has traveled throughout these United States and abroad to nine other countries for ministry in word and song. 23,000 souls were led to the Lord in Pakistan alone.

2017 and 2018 recipient of the Gulf Coast Gospel Music Awards. Performed recently to 40,000 people at Lakewood Church in Houston, Texas with Sir the Baptist and Churchppl.

DOROTHY WILSON

Discover the Greatness Within You
Dorothy Wilson

Over the past five years, I've made an unbelievable number of new connections. Thousands of women would say, "I know her!" But, you know what, most of them really don't know me. They know of me.

To really know me, you'd need to take a long walk back into my past. I would have to take you back before we could go forward. Let's travel

beyond my present time as a very successful entrepreneur and community leader who is inspiring the nation. Let's go beyond those years as a newspaper journalist. Beyond those years at University of Georgia. Beyond those years as a scholar in high school. Now let's go even further to the time when I was 8 years old, living in a wooden shack of a house situated in the middle of crops my Daddy worked for a living.

GROWING UP

Growing up, I watched my father physically and verbally abuse my mother and siblings over and over. Weekends were the worst.

So many nights, I was startled awake because my alcoholic dad had a gun to my mom's head or stomach, snarling "I'll kill you."

I also have memories of running through the woods barefoot, as bullets sliced through the limbs and trees, barely missing us. I still freak out at the sound of a gun firing.

My siblings ran away one by one by the time they reached age 12 or so. They couldn't endure the pain anymore.

HAND TIED, MOUTH SHUT

I felt as though my hands were tied behind my back and my mouth was taped shut. I was helpless, hopeless to help my mother, my sisters and brothers.

Every young child fears an imaginary monster in the closet or under the bed. In my case, that monster was alive, breathing — and an accurate shooter. He was very real and he wasn't hiding.

Even after my mother escaped, taking us with her, I lived in constant fear — and I was angry. Very angry. I was angry that I couldn't do anything to change my circumstances. I was angry because I believe my mother to be a coward. I was angry and confused because Daddy was a wonderful person — smart, handsome, full of laughter, hard-working, generous to others — until he started drinking.

These ugly experiences bound me in a prison of fear, rejection and unforgiveness for many years.

By my late 20s, I had completed college (the first in my family to achieve a higher education), landed a job with good pay, married and birthed two sons. I seemed so successful. But inside, I remained trapped by my past. I longed for more meaning in my life. After surviving so much hell, there had to be more than career achievement, a husband and kids.

I began seeking that more. And what I found was a God who loved me and had his own definition of who I was. I was not my college degree, job title or someone's wife. For the first time, I began to understand that I was the daughter of the master of the universe. Daughter!!!!!

I remember the day I was reading in the book of Psalms and came across this scripture: "Keep me as the apple of the eye, hide me under the shadow of thy wings."

Ever had one of those moments where you're stopped in your tracks? Well, that is exactly what happened! I backed up and said to myself, "I'm the apple of His eye and I can hide behind Him."

I felt truly safe for the first time in my life! And the revelation of who I am in Christ just began to reverberate and reverberate and reverberate. It was as if He were erasing all of the negativity, the anger, the tears, the hurt. I was NOT defined by what happened to me and my family. I was NOT an angry woman. I was NOT a fearful woman. I was the daughter of a KING!

NOW

So now we're ready to talk about a Trailblazer Who Leads. To value my voice and my perspective, you had to know where it comes from.

This new woman was ready to run toward her destiny and achieve something special — not to show everyone else that she wasn't a little poor country girl with a ugly secret. Nooooo, she now was ready to walk forward seeing a King as her father, and as His daughter, she had every right to expect to achieve greatness and overcome every obstacle.

But you know, life's just not that easy, is it? Ha! I came to realize that those struggles were just my edu-ma-cation so I could overcome the many other battles that were ahead.

LAYOFF TO LAYUP

My life seemed to take off as I walked in my newness. Everytime I walked into my boss' office, he was ready to offer a raise. I landed a job with an award-winning kick-butt team at a South Carolina newspaper. I was offered executive leadership training and hopped from that right into a managing editor job handling a million-plus budget and news coverage for the Mississippi Coast region. I was helping to drive success in my company.

I later created a team that others in the company begged to become a part of. I took the company's special projects division to new heights. I helped to create a magazine that was named Best in the State four years in a row. I managed a post-Katrina book that became a New York Times bestseller. What could stop me now?

Huh. God's plan can stop you. It was time for me to leave newspapers, but I was too scared to leave my salary and benefits. After spending 28 years in the publishing business, I was laid off. I was just ONE rung away from wearing the crown of publisher when my ladder crashed to the floor.

EXHALE

Seems I should have been angry, tearful, hurt. But deep inside of me, there was an excitement building. I tasted more.

You see, that corporate job was just another box that had encased me.

I had become someone that I really didn't want to be. Very successful by every one else's definition but feeling empty and compromised inside.

What was I doing?

What had happened to my passion to give voice to others who were unempowered and uninformed? Wasn't that the reason I got that degree in journalism?

Some of you reading these pages may find yourself asking similar questions. When you look at the authors in the this book, you see success, success, success. But each of us have a story to tell of trials and failure.

Here's the difference between those who achieve greatness and those who don't: The ones who find it find themselves first. If you keep pouring into others from just your skills and experience and not your passion, you'll run out of good stuff to pour.

Go back to what inspired you in the first place. Because I saw my mother be held back, muzzled, I knew I had to help other women find their voice, find their destiny. And within that passion, lies my greatness.

When I transformed my thinking about who I was and what defined me, I was then able to renovate my life and change my trajectory. You've heard the saying, "as a woman thinketh, so is she."

TRANSFORM

Transform your thinking, transform your life. You see, you are not your job title. You are not what others say you are. Your past doesn't have to define you. You are as big and bad as you're able to think and dream. I love it when Gloria Mayfield Banks says, "Super Bad All Day Long!" I got the T-shirt, girl!

I'm not a journalist. I'm not a magazine publisher. I'm not a marketing consultant. No, I'm an empowerment coach who knows something about succeeding in business, developing marketing strategies and so on and so on. You get my point.

Instead of having tape over my mouth and my hands bound behind my back, feeling powerless, I am now speaking from a very loud platform called Gulf Coast Woman Magazine and am empowering hundreds of women everyday.

I have switched lanes from struggling to find my way to helping other women find their lane and run faster. And I do that EVERY DAY. What it looks like on the outside is publishing two very popular women's magazines in print and online; operating a regional division of a national marketing firm; co-founding and co-directing a Top 10 Professional Women's Conference; coaching and mentoring other women who lead in my church; inspiring other women, particularly women of color in my community, that they can have a seat and a voice at the table.

It also looks like expanding my reach from a city, to my state and to the nation. One of my proudest moments was being named one of 25 Top African-Americans in the state of Mississippi. I'm also proud to be called "Madam President" when I walk into the boardroom of the Mississippi Gulf Coast Chamber of Commerce.

Enough about me. Now, what about you? It's time to step off into the real you — step off into a place where fear doesn't hold you. Step off into fulfillment that fuels your soul and uncaps your potential.

Light yourself on fire! Be all you were created to be. And then set some other people on fire!

If you're looking for opportunity, you will find it.

If you're looking in the rearview mirror, you'll miss everything in the windshield in front of you.

Wake up each day asking: "God, what would you have me do today? I have greatness within me."

Say it and believe it, "I have greatness within me!"

About Dorothy Wilson

Dorothy Patrick Wilson is a brand strategist, coach, speaker and author who empowers women to step off their place of comfort into the real version of themselves. A Southern girl, she publishes magazines, hosts podcasts and co-directs the Success Women's Conference, a top 10 conference for professional women in the U.S. Achievements she's most proud of include serving as president of the Mississippi Gulf Coast Chamber of Commerce; being named SBA Women Business Champion of the Year for the state of Mississippi; receiving the Pat Santucci Spirit of the Coast trophy, One Coast Community Leader award, Tom Tandler Lifetime Achievement Award and MHA Humanitarian of the Year Award; and being named 1 of 25 Top African-Americans in the State of Mississippi. Her books include "Little Book of Weapons: How to Defeat Your Giants" and "Unboxed: 25 Women Break Free & Soar".

GENEVA DUMMER

Adapt and Overcome: Resiliency is the Key to Survival
Geneva Dummer

There I was - a new mother with a new job, desperately looking for a way to combine both. This was the umpteenth time I've had to rebrand or take on unfamiliar responsibilities - nothing new there. I was looking forward to the challenge of both awesome responsibilities, yet reluctant to give up either. I've always tied my identity to what I do. I like to feel useful - it gives me a sense of accomplishment. I always did well in school, but really enjoyed working, which was good because money was tight - my mom was a single woman with two children. I held two jobs during high school in addition to being in marching, concert and jazz bands. I was co-drum major my senior year and joined the concert choir and show choirs. That was also the year I performed in my first play. My senior year was one of trying new things - I was all about "why not?"

After I graduated, I asked if I could transfer my job at Sunglass Hut to San Antonio. My request was approved so at 17 I packed up the car and moved with my cats and a boyfriend. I took over his apartment lease and worked at Sunglass Hut and Olive Garden (because a girl's got to eat, right?) for a year and then decided I needed something a little more stable. I visited all the recruiters and decided the U.S. Navy was the right choice and not a difficult one, since my father and grandfather were both also in the Navy. My recruiter wisely advised me to enlist for four years rather than the two I had originally planned, which allowed me to receive a rate (job designation) once I completed initial school. Having personally seen and heard about the dreaded "undesignated" status, I can't thank him enough! I completed all the training necessary and was designated an Avionics Technician (AT), going through a more specialized school geared toward circuit board repair, which also allowed me to increase my rank.

I loved being in the Navy and highly recommend the experience to anyone. Sure, there were good times and bad, but that's just life, isn't it? Overall, the seven years I spent serving our country were extremely beneficial. Beyond learning a valuable trade, I learned a lot about what I and other people were capable of – the good, the bad, and the ugly. I worked my way up from technician to inspector, to shop supervisor, to quality assurance, and then was ready for a change. I had always been interested in the medical field. Being enlisted, the only cross-rate opportunity was corpsman. Unfortunately, that rate had no openings. I looked at possibly applying for officer or warrant officer, but I really felt it was time to move on, so I opted not to reenlist, packed my seabag and my cats and headed back home - hoping to eventually go to college.

Since I was the first in my immediate family to go to college, I wasn't quite sure what the process was to enroll. I knew I'd need money, so I went back to work to add to my very small savings account - this time as a property manager at a storage facility. I learned a lot, but didn't make much. Along the way, I met the man I would eventually marry and have children with. I had no intention at the time of getting married OR having children, but I enjoyed his company and he seemed to be okay with my independent (stubborn) nature. He suggested I might join him at school in Wyoming and offered a small scholarship at the community college where he was completing his degree. We partnered in a fierce parliamentary debate team and my college career was finally, officially, underway.

He graduated with an associate degree and we headed off to state college together. I needed to wait another six months before I could transfer, so I went back to work – this time as an optician. I passed the certification test and enjoyed the work. By the time I went back to school, I had worked long enough to enjoy a little flexibility in my schedule, allowing me to take a full course load each semester. I began preparing for medical school and majored in molecular biology with a computer science minor. Along the way, I added a job with the USDA in one of their campus laboratories under my first mentor and, again, I couldn't have been luckier. I also realized I'd rather work in research finding solutions as opposed to treating the same symptoms with no solution in sight. As I moved into upper level classes, I realized I needed to drop the computer science minor but I was proud of what I had accomplished and glad to have the associated knowledge. It served me well in graduate school, where I built on that skill set with DNA and protein analysis/modeling programs, as well as general program knowledge. My time in the Navy built a solid base in troubleshooting problems and this also allowed me to do some really good work under yet another amazing woman.

As I progressed in my studies, so did my partner in life. After four years in Wyoming, he agreed to settle somewhere that did not guarantee freezing cold temperatures more months of the year than not and he also loves being near water as much as I do. He went on to law school and I was accepted into a PhD program, where I was able to study gene therapy. Only one university near his law school offered this field of study at the time, which was the only program I applied to. We happily immersed ourselves in our respective fields of study. Upon graduating from law school, he accepted a job with a reputable firm in a place near the water that rarely sees snow or freezing temperatures. Unfortunately, it also offered nothing in the way of post-doctoral opportunities in gene therapy. This rebranding was, and still is, difficult to take. I could have commuted to one of three nearby cities and worked in a lab doing similar work, but research from a distance is not ideal and we also began thinking in earnest about starting a family - not an ideal situation for lab life, as there are no holidays or vacations or much in the way of time off at all. Not that I minded - I would work all day every day given the chance, especially in my chosen field, but the time had come to consider the larger picture. I left the program with a master's degree and a husband to set about finding yet another job.

I learned about an opportunity as a department head in human resources through one of the ladies at my husband's firm and retooled my resume to address what I could find about human resources, applying the skills I had to the ones I'd need to do the job. I bought a suit and headed into my first interview as an administrative professional. Thankfully, I made a good impression and was offered the position in what turned out to be another fantastic learning experience. I was able to implement several improvements and discovered a new flavor in my already developed knack for finding solutions. I enjoyed the work and most of the people I worked with. I even challenged myself to face my fear of public speaking by auditioning for and performing in community theater. After about a year and a half, we decided to add our first child to the mix.

This brings me back to the beginning of this chapter as a new mother with a new job. I should also mention about a year after I began working in HR my husband added a new business to our lives - a used car lot. After the baby was born, he asked if I'd come on board as HR manager and bookkeeper. Never being one to turn down a learning opportunity, I accepted the challenge and I could not have jumped any further out of the frying pan! To say the least, I developed a very thorough and intimate understanding of bookkeeping and business operations in all sorts of interesting scenarios. I needed to work from home most days just to keep distractions and interruptions to a minimum, but home also had its own set of distractions and interruptions with a baby in the house. This conundrum (and the addition of another child three years later) inspired me to consider how productivity and parenting can coexist in the workplace and I continue to work toward that goal while also helping others to achieve their potential in the process.

About Geneva Dummer

GENEVA'S MISSION is to help people achieve their goals efficiently and effectively. With over 30 years of experience spanning several different industries, she pays great attention to detail while maintaining view of the comprehensive picture. Her priorities are economic development, public health, and community development.

Geneva was born in Florida and joined the Navy in 1992. She proudly served 7 years as an Avionics Technician, Collateral Duty Inspector, and finally Quality Assurance Inspector. She earned her B.S. in Molecular Biology at the University of Wyoming and her Master of Science Degree at the University of Tennessee.

Geneva currently lives in Biloxi with her husband, Stephen, and their 2 children. She has served on numerous boards of directors of nonprofit organizations and enjoys performing occasionally with local community theater groups. She serves as Administrator of Heritage Trails Partnership of the Mississippi Gulf Coast and opened The Meeting Place in 2016.

HEATHER EASON

It All Started with a Beer

Heather Eason

My sister has always supported my crazy ideas and this time was no different. Maybe it was silly, but we were going to do it anyway.

It was 2016 and the news was filled with tragic stories of homes flooding in what they called a "500-year" storm. The images of waterlogged houses and distraught survivors resonated deep in my soul. It brought me back to the day Hurricane Katrina visited my home as an unwelcome guest. As her waters slowly crept into our home, we frantically worked to save all we could. We sent my twelve-year-old son upstairs when the water reached our ankles. In an instant the storm became angrier and the floodwaters came in faster. Suddenly, saving our stuff didn't matter – saving our lives did.

I looked down the hallway and saw the closed bedroom door. My husband was in that room. The water was now almost to my waist and it was steadily rising. I shouted for him to pull the door and he shouted for me to push. There was no moving it. I tried harder but my legs had no strength against the force of nature's fury. My desperate screams were muffled only by the thoughts racing through my head - thoughts of having to tell his children their dad drowned and I couldn't save him, although he was just inches away; thoughts of my son being upstairs and how I could rescue him; thoughts of the skiff tied to the tree. My thoughts turned to prayers. I traveled to the pits of despair and with a broken heart, removed my hands from the door so I could go upstairs to save my son.

God was merciful and replaced my hands with His. Suddenly, the entire door broke loose and my husband and I were swept down the hall on an indoor wave filled with furniture and dirt and photos and shit. The septic mess brought us to the stair railing and we made it to the second floor. The phone signals were jammed but I was able to make a call to my sister. I told her the water was coming in, that we didn't know how we were going to make it out…then the signal died. To this day, that call haunts Aimee. She

63

waited in agony for hours and hours not knowing if we were alive or dead. Although it wasn't on purpose, it's the worst thing I've ever done to her.

In the eye of the storm, we made our escape.

My best friend, Mindy, opened the door and found us covered in water and sewage. We were a mess, but we were alive. She and Randy housed us for over three weeks.

The day after the storm, my husband told me he wanted to cook everything in our restaurant and give it away. I felt like I could fall back in love with him and I did…for a while. Fundamental differences and the fury of the storm left our marriage on the rocks. We eventually divorced, but at the time we focused on recovery.

The day after Katrina, we started cooking everything in the restaurant. It took days to give it all away. Trucks of supplies arrived before the Red Cross, so our back parking lot became a makeshift distribution center. The work was constant but taking a break wasn't an option.

My mom was coming from Colorado but the trip in the U-Haul was brutal. A week had passed when she arrived. She looked as tired as we were. Everyone's minds and bodies were exhausted but something cool was getting ready to happen. Mom opened the back of the U-Haul to a large cooler filled with ice cold beer. After a week of working in the sizzling sun we popped the tops. There were eight of us.

Together, we stood behind that U-Haul and drank something cold, something that wasn't water, something that was …a treat. In my entire life, I'll never again drink anything that good. I believe Homer would have referred to it as "the nectar of the Gods".

It was a combination of that drink of beer in 2005 and a trip to Denham Springs in 2016 that birthed what would become a "pay it forward" movement called Comeback Coolers.

As I mentioned earlier, the Denham Springs flood really hit home. I'd experienced the water and the emotional toll it inflicted so I felt compelled to go. People eagerly donated cleaning supplies and hygiene items.

With the truck packed, I traveled to Denham Springs with a "can do" attitude. I rounded a corner and saw the first pile of household items. Immediately, I started sobbing like a child. *Pull it together, Heather, you can't let these people see you like this,* I thought.

I wiped my eyes and waited for the red to drain out of my face before driving into the neighborhood.

Just like the days after Katrina, people were working to clean up their homes. Neighbors were helping each other. No one waited on the government. It was people helping people.

It didn't take long to pass out the supplies. I knew I'd be back. On my way home, I asked myself what I appreciated most after my home flooded. Over and over, my mind went back to that day my mom brought the beer.

Beer. I was going to bring beer.

I called my sister.

I started asking people for their used coolers, beer, drinks, oranges, and baby wipes. At our first packing party I stopped people who were passing by and asked them to sign coolers and add words of encouragement. We collected and filled twenty-five Comeback Coolers!

Aimee and I strapped everything down to a borrowed trailer and headed to Louisiana.

I'll admit, it was kind of weird approaching the first person. But, boy oh boy was he glad to see us! Aimee and I were as overwhelmed as the recipients. They had received food, cleaning supplies, and all the tangible things necessary after a storm but it was the care and concern sent to them by everyone involved in the coolers that brought hope, compassion, and love. We didn't know it then, but God was working in a huge way.

In 2017, Texas was pounded by Hurricane Harvey. Two of our local artists, Craig and Matt, got involved and raised over $5,000 toward the effort. People volunteered, donated, and helped us collect and fill over 200 coolers at our second packing party. A Denham Springs recipient, Amber, started her own campaign and began the "pay it forward" movement. We picked up thirty coolers from her on our way to Vidor, Texas.

We were welcomed in Texas the same way we were in Louisiana. The Comeback Coolers team witnessed people's resilience and we shared pictures of them on Facebook. Donors looked on Facebook to see who received the cooler they sent – they could literally see where their donations were going and people liked that.

A few weeks later we brought another 150 coolers to Middleburg, FL, and added Kids Comeback Coolers. From that point on, every child we saw received their own cooler filled with snacks and toys.

The 2018 storm season was unyielding but, again, people wanted to help. We received a call from a woman in Vidor who wanted to "pay it forward" but we weren't headed in that direction. Bob Conley got involved to make it work. Britni's campaign yielded well over 150 coolers for North Carolina. Combined with the Mississippi and Louisiana efforts, we brought 250 Comeback Coolers and seventy kids' coolers to Lake Waccamaw and Crusoe Island.

Two weeks later, four North Carolina recipients, whose homes were still damaged, collected coolers and joined us to deliver more that 250 Comeback Coolers to Socastee, South Carolina.

Later that season, Hurricane Michael reared his ugly head and slammed into Florida as a category 5 hurricane. Now, all hands were on deck.

Louisiana, Texas, Mississippi, and the Carolinas collectively gathered and distributed over 500 Comeback Coolers to Altha, Panama City, and Lynn Haven.

Two years after our first delivery of twenty-five coolers, we delivered over 1,000 hard-back coolers, 100 kids' coolers, and 20 lineman's buckets to three states.

It all happened because people paid it forward.

As I write this, I'm in the passenger seat of the Comeback Coolers truck. We're on our way to tornado-devastated Nashville. We've never worked a tornado before, but we can't sit idle.

School kids, teenagers, church groups, families, senior citizens, and a country super star signed and designed coolers, supplied items, and donated money. Many of them will look at the pictures we post and will be able to see who received the cooler they sent.

When Nashville recovers, they will step up and help another community. And the trend will continue. It's always been about people helping people.

And to think, it all started with a beer.

About Heather Eason

Heather Abigail Eason is the Founder of the nationally recognized non-profit organization, Comeback Coolers. The organization, which has delivered thousands of filled coolers to disaster survivors, is fueled by everyone involved who has turned it into a pay-it-forward movement.

Heather has been featured in MS Gulf Coast Magazine, South Mississippi Strong, and on Nettye Johnson's Faith Applied podcast. She has received the Key to the City of Ocean Springs, was nominated as Hero of the Year by the Lions Club, honored as Grand Marshal of the Elks Parade, and won the prestigious Hardee's All-Star award.

Among other things, she was a high school drop-out and teen mother but fought against the statistics. Those struggles fuel her desire to make the world a cooler place.

Today, she holds a Master's Degree, has created several community programs, and enjoys the love and encouragement of God, her adult children, family, friends, and Bob.

JACQUELINE MCKEEVER

Out of Darkness

Jacqueline Mckeever

My name is Jacqueline McKeever . You can call me Jackie. I'm a Life and Business Coach. I help entrepreneurs build their life, finances, and their business. I have a MBA and a minor in Accounting. I'm an expert in business planning and management. The thing I'm most proud of besides being a mom of three adults is freeing myself of 204k of debt, overcoming depression, boldly standing in my purpose, and helping others overcome limited beliefs that lead to connecting to their purpose. You may have thought while reading the title, "What in the world is she talking about?" What I mean when I'm talking about "dark" is depression. In this section of the book I will talk about what depression is. I will mention a couple of different types of depression some I experienced and some I have not. Then I will tell you when I was able to leave the darkness and step into the light.

When I think about this time, the study of depression was not familiar or known to me as it is today. Many people would say in the '80s and '90s that people who claimed they were depressed chose to be, or that they were crazy. I've even heard people say that the people were just lazy. And these assumptions are very, very far from the truth.

Depression is a mood disorder that causes persistent feelings of loss and sadness. It can affect the way you feel, think, causes weakness, and can make you withdraw from normal day to day activities. When I felt clinical depression, I felt trapped deep inside a dark space within myself. At first, I could fake the funk and pretend like there was nothing wrong. Then one day, the weight of it got so heavy that it hurt to breathe.

There are several different types of depression. I will only go over a few common types and the couple I faced. One type that is common to people living in places like Alaska, where there are several months of darkness. It is known as Seasonal Affective Disorder (SAD). Often, people diagnosed with this experience relief simply by being in an area where they are exposed to sunlight for longer periods.

Postpartum depression and Situation depression are the two things that led to me having major or clinical depression. In 1997, I gave birth to a son. After his birth I was so depressed. I couldn't hide it and I didn't know what it was. I was suffering from Postpartum depression. You see, during this time primary many OBGYN's were not as focused on the mental health of the mom as they are now. It turned into a Situation depression after my son's death. Situation depression is the result of an extremely stressful life-event or series of events leading to significant changes in a person's life. It took me 12 years before I could even say my son's name without bursting into tears.

If I'm totally honest, I do have a part to play in all my bouts with depression. You see, I was hiding. I would shrink to make others feel as though they were superior or smarter to make them feel better about themselves so they will leave me alone. I never spoke about how anything made me feel unless I was angry. During all those events I was hiding. I hid because I didn't value myself. I feared my own power. I believed the lie my environment told me. I believed the lie told by those around me and their behaviors. I began to tell myself the same lie. So my talent, my power and my appointment stayed dormant until one day it didn't.

I remember the night the darkness did not prevail over my life. I had a dream one day. I dreamed I spoke to the Holy Spirit on a bridge. I stood on a bridge contemplating whether or not to jump. All I could think about is how I wanted to stop hurting. The Holy Spirit in the dream told me to live. When I asked how it replied to stop hiding. I asked for more. The reply was, "If you give me more, I will show you more". I replied I will. I woke up and the dark spirit was broken. It was literally a "come to Jesus" moment in my life I will never forget. The dream represented my need to no longer hide and the desire for approval. I gave myself permission to live as my authentic self. So I began getting treatment for depression.

Now, this next part of the story may not be your solution. I went from being medicated and seeing my therapist every week to not requiring medication and only seeing them as needed (PRN). I learned I must walk purposefully, be the authentic, and the high-energy person God created me to be. The more I worked on me, the stronger I grew. I grew stronger vibration, thoughts, words, my behavior, and by deciding to release. Two of my favorite scriptures that really put into words my experience are John 5:1-14 and Ezekiel 37:1-14.

It's the reason I choose to call myself a Life and Business Coach and discuss the connection between you and your purpose. It involves making the decision to let go of limiting beliefs and breathe life into dry bones. This causes them to not only live but to thrive. This period I was in the light. During my healing process I created a non-profit called Route to Victory, where I spread the message that you are a Victorious Warrior and money cannot overcome you. Then as time went on, my voice became stronger and I created Jackie McKeever, LLC. In this entity, I help entrepreneurs build their lives, finances, and their business. I do this by teaching, coaching, and consulting them in areas of business planning, business management, client attraction, and growth and stability life coaching. I teach them to stand strong and firm on the power they were given. I teach them to remove the doubts so they can be victorious. I teach that it starts with wanting to. Their gift was not created just for them. They hold the solution to someone's issue. It's all about connection. Out of darkness came the light. That light continues to shine in me and through me as I walk in God's light. Connect with me by going to:www.jackiemckeever.com/contactus.   Take the leap and let's build!

About Jacqueline Mckeever

Jackie McKeever is a Life and Business Coach. She creates growth strategies that help Christian women thrive in the areas of personal development, personal finance, and business planning & management.

She has an MBA with a minor in accounting, she has over 20 years of experience supporting others to be their best in the Corporate World. She freed herself of 204k of debt, found the courage to pursue her vision, her purpose, launched her business, and got the support I need to do it well. Her journey began when she broke free of depression and became a financial coach to a nonprofit. That lead her to create a profit business called Jackie McKeever LLC. She helps people connect to their own why and harness their gifts and purpose to excel.

She has spoken at churches, podcasts, summits, corporate, nonprofit groups, etc. She helps people excel in "faith to the boardroom".

JANELL EDWARDS

Having Fun, Failing Forward!

Janell Edwards

Have you ever asked yourself, "how in the hell did I get here?!" Married, robbing Peter to pay Paul, robbing Peter and Paul, a victim of domestic violence, divorced, married and divorced again (to the same man), single mother of three children, on public assistance, homeless, close to a nervous breakdown, overweight, isolated…I mean really, I was raised in a two-parent home; attended private school from first to twelfth grade; received a Savannah State College (SSC - now Savannah State University) scholarship, where I played on the SSC volleyball team; was captain of the flag corps in the SSC marching band; a SSC peer counselor; pledged Delta Sigma Theta Sorority; a member of the Newtonian Society; inducted into Phi Beta Kappa Honor Society; became Miss Savannah State College 1989-90, graduated Cum Laude with a Bachelor of Science degree in Mathematics with a minor in Computer Science; received a full scholarship to Michigan State University grad school; a board certified licensed cosmetologist; owner of a salon and mobile day spa; and a mathematics teacher. Again, "how in the HELL did I get here?!"

I believe the answer lies in the mystery surrounding the emotional abyss of complexities encompassed in this simple word: 'relationship.' At this juncture in my life of a mere 51 years young, I have come to acknowledge that many of the decisions and choices I've made were mostly determined by the weight of pressure I felt due to relationships with others - my family, my friends, my professors, my husband, my children, my God (based on other's interpretation of Him), society and the like. Everyone except myself! Now, by how my youth and collegiate years sound, it may seem that listening and heeding everyone else's advice to the letter led me down the right path. Looking good on the outside - college-educated, well-dressed, secure job, a husband, children, a nice new whip (Lincoln Navigator), quarter of a million-dollar home in a cul-de-sac on Wilmington Island, and a business entrepreneur. But I didn't realize the transformation taking place inwardly was a spiritual cancer filled with stress, feelings of inadequacy, doubt, undo pressure, and a false sense of appearing 'right'. I didn't fully understand that the most significant and influential connection I only needed to focus on was the **relationship with myself**. I believe when we arrive in the earthly realm as infants we are bestowed with gifts and talents from God above, but then as we begin to matriculate through the years of being a toddler, to pre-adolescents, to adolescence, to teens and on into adulthood, we are inundated and programmed with generational precepts developed and passed down in our families and derived from the time period where our great grandparents, grandparents, and parents are beholden. We then succumb to the preconceived ideologies and fall in line and dance to the beat of the prescribed societal drum until we return to the spiritual realm from whence we came.

So what does this have to do with my Trailblazer experience and having fun, failing forward? For all intents and purposes, when I started to govern my life, by rebirthing the relationship with **my true spiritual self** (for "we are not human beings having a spiritual experience, we are spiritual beings having a human experience" - Pierre Teilhard de Chardin), it looked to those around me as if I was off my rocker, losing my mind, just plain *failing*, but to *me*, I was *having fun*!

Therefore, listening to my inner being is governed by two questions that must be answered in the affirmative simultaneously - and they are: 1) Does it feel good to me? And 2) Is it working out for me? If I answer these two questions and the answer is 'yes' to both at the same time, I'm traveling down that highway, full speed ahead! But if it felt good to me but did not work out for me then I'm taking the very next exit and vice versa.

I say all this because we really don't realize when we're not connected to our true spiritual inner being and understand the God-given purpose in which we are here to fulfill. We're literally the walking dead, a zombie, a shadow of the true spiritual man housed inside this dust-built house we call bodies. As I began to truly connect and understand MY God, I understood that as my natural family members, friends, husband, children, and others did not understand and looked at me like I was losing my mind, making serious mistakes, wasting precious time, not being a good wife and mother (sentiments of my two-time ex-husband), just not knowing what I'm doing, and frankly in *failing* I realized I was just starting to understand what I am here to do and that's to have some FUN!

Listening to my inner being made me enroll in the Projections School of Beauty and pass state boards to attain a master cosmetologist license; become a salon owner and successful network marketer; resign from my teaching position in the Chatham County school system; move from Savannah, Georgia, to Ferriday, Louisiana, and then to Fayette, Mississippi, with my children; marry Anthony Edwards (the man My God made for me); become a community engagement specialist and the Executive Director of award-winning grassroots nonprofit organization Fayette Community Service Organization (FCSO) who own WWGI 101.5 LPFM radio station in southwest Mississippi; become a radio and social media personality, Jazzy J; become an event/program planner; become a grant writer and public speaker; become co-owner of pecan shelling company WeCan Pecan in Jefferson County, Mississippi; become a farmer and establish a farmer's market in rural Mississippi; and lose over 100 pounds and maintain it for over 9 years to become the co-creator of FCSO's FAT to Fit Olympic Games - an event that will eradicate the silent epidemic of childhood obesity!

I remember holding the acclaimed Heavyweight Champion title of EVENT DIETING for 20 years! My friend (I will just call her Renee), was my tag team member who religiously engaged on every fad diet endeavor to get us ready for the next big social event such as homecoming festivities, a girl's road trip, or simply to fit into that outfit we purchased where the zipper just didn't quite reach the top. We would always start on a Monday after we gorged ourselves on beloved high-calorie southern comfort food at a quite famous buffet in Savannah on Sunday afternoons. We would call this our 'last supper' before we started trim-fast, slim-fast, the 3-day diet, the lemonade diet, the boiled egg diet, the cabbage soup diet, the low-carb diet and so many other diet plans that eventually gave the same results - getting into the outfit, looking fabulous and slayed for the event, and then putting all the weight back on plus a few more pounds. This spiraling cycle of yo-yo weight loss and weight gain continued from 1990 to 2010!

79

My family and I moved from Ferriday, Louisiana, to Fayette, Mississippi, in 2009. Unbeknownst to me, Mississippi was researched as the most obese state in the nation and Jefferson County in particular was the most obese county. We learned this disheartening fact as FCSO started a program entitled, "The Seed to the Need Project", where we taught area youth how to plant, nurture, and harvest a fruit or vegetables and create a value-added product to sell. Our focus was teaching entrepreneurism to establish and maintain economic sustainability in the 17th poorest county in the nation. However, when we were picked up by the local news station, the story was broadcast as the "fattest county in the nation is teaching their youth about nutrition." This news was revelatory to me to say the least! I remember sitting on the couch and screaming at top of my lungs "ARE WE THE MOST OBESE COUNTY IN MISSISSIPPI?!" My mother-in-law, who I affectionately call Mama Dee, handed me a Jackson Mississippi newspaper, the Clarion Ledger, July 14, 2004 edition and big Joe, my husband's older brother, was pictured on the front page in an article stating that Jefferson County was researched as the "fattest county in America." Shortly after the news broadcast, my husband and I attended the Global Obesity Summit (GOS) held in Jackson, MS, to find out more information on the effects of obesity on our rural-impoverished, food-desert, vulnerable community.

The GOS was a huge eye-opener for me on how obesity detrimentally affects us as a society and more importantly how it will affect our future generations. Doctors attended from 34 various countries from around the globe. While I didn't fully understand the overwhelming technical terminology, I left with three facts that changed my life: 1) due to the chronic conditions brought on by obesity, the lifespan of our children would potentially be cut by 12 years; 2) childhood obesity effects African American youth at a 51% higher prevalence rate than any other ethnicity; and 3) we are living in an age where parents will bury their children due to the chronic conditions brought on by obesity. Hence, the creation of the FAT to Fit Olympic Games (FTFOG) event. The FTFOG is an event engaging youth and adults to have amazing fun and laughter while improving their health through playing fun games, participating in free health screenings, and winning great prizes! Over the past 9 years we have conducted 15,789 free health screenings on community residents, engaged participants from 13 Mississippi counties and 5 US states nationwide, and awarded over 1,000 new bicycles and over $5,000 in cash and health gear prizes! WE ARE THE INSPIRATION FOR THE NATION, FIGHTING OBESITY!

Thank you for taking time out of your precious day to read my story of having fun, failing forward! My prayer is that some aspect of my journey will inspire yours and we will all matriculate to the next level of GREATNESS for our personal life purpose and path.

About Janell Edwards

Janell Edwards is a born leader, humanitarian, and inspiration specialist. Driven by compassion and love she takes supreme confidence in providing the best thought-provoking knowledge possible to focus her listeners to achieve the next level of greatness for their lives.

As a mathematician, master cosmetologist, make-up artist, event planner, live radio/social media talk show host, public speaker, entrepreneur, painter, designer, crafter, gardener, farmer and executive director of an award-winning non-profit organization, her goals are to share her experiences with other young men and women (including youth) to convey knowledge that will help them to discover the gems of golden gifts and talents that our Creator has hidden deep down in THEIR very soul! In the parable of the talents, even the servant with the one talent could have doubled it, only if he/she knew THEIR TRUE SPIRITUAL SELF!

KIMAKA BOWENS

From Tragedy to Triumph
Kimaka Bowens

We don't come into this world knowing our purpose, but there is a purpose attached to our lives. I was born out of ashes: the product of rape. Throughout my childhood I hated I didn't feel loved. I hated I didn't trust. I hated I felt a sense of emptiness. I hated I didn't feel protected. I hated I wasn't someone else. I hated myself.

I can remember portions of my childhood as though they occurred yesterday, because during a portion of my elementary school years I was molested by my stepfather. My mother was unable to help because she was enduring her own horror. My stepfather drank heavily and he was abusive towards my mother. I remember the stale feeling of being unloved. I felt a sense of loneliness words can't explain. If you stood at the edge of the Grand Canyon and threw out a penny, who would search for it? I was that penny.

No child should have their childhood stolen from them and replaced with pain and dark memories. A particular emergency room visit still plays vividly in my mind. "If you do this again, we will have to pump your stomach. Don't do this again," said a nurse in the emergency room as she scolded me over my suicide attempt. I sat on an examining table with severe stomach cramps while vomiting from the handful of Tylenol I had ingested hours earlier. My grandmother consoled me as she tried to make sense of why her 13-year old granddaughter would try to kill herself. The nurse, seemingly cold, reminded me of everything I wanted to escape in this world.

By 10th grade I was pregnant and ashamed of myself. I had my son at 16 years old and, determined to succeed, I graduated from high school and enrolled in junior college. Months later I quit, but I later re-enrolled with a stronger sense of commitment...I quit again. Finally, I enrolled in a medical assistant program in the mid '90s. In an unexpected turn of events, I stared at a pregnancy test thinking this could not be my reality. I was pregnant, again. The thought of having two children on my income was unfathomable. I decided an abortion was the best option. As I lay in bed the night after the abortion, I was terrorized by the cry of a baby who wasn't there. I pleaded with God to take this pain from me and I pledged not to have another abortion.

I was able to complete the program and I began working as a medical assistant at a family practice. I lived in Section-8 housing and receiving food stamps when my life changed - I was pregnant once again. Honoring the promise I made to God, I decided to carry my baby to term. However, I believed adoption was the most logical decision because I only made minimum wage. After a difficult pregnancy, I changed my mind and decided I was strong enough to parent two children. I can tell you that being a pregnant, unwed African American had its challenges within the doctor's office. I recall asking my OB about a pediatrician for my daughter. He glanced at my record and saw "Medicaid" and in a snarky tone responded, "Well, I pay for your baby to be born." I immediately reminded him that even at 21 years old and without a husband, I still worked. I guess he was surprised to learn we were "splitting the cost."

To ensure I wouldn't have any more children, I spoke with my doctor about a tubal ligation. I remember that conversation as if it were yesterday. "I would like a tubal ligation," I told my doctor. "No! You're too young," he said. "Sir, I don't want to be on Medicaid for the rest of my life. If I continue having children they will become lifetime dependents of welfare." My doctor granted the tubal ligation.

I will never know what changed his mind. Perhaps he was a proponent of women's rights, or perhaps the vision of a poor black woman with 10 kids standing in line at the grocery store with him was enough to make him consent. One will never know.

I needed a plan of action. I learned about a program which incentivized learning by funding transportation while providing child care assistance. I enrolled in a Licensed Practical Nursing program where I graduated as Valedictorian. I was going to be an example of hard work for my children and prove the naysayers wrong. While working a shift, I mentioned to an RN my desire to continue my education. Instead of encouragement, she reminded me how difficult the RN program was: "much more strenuous than the LPN track."Maybe she was right, so I convinced myself I couldn't possibly complete an RN program. I started to tune into the narrative others had for me, and their narratives became fuel for my drive. God reminded me that He authored my story, not them. In Romans 5:3-4 Paul says "…and endurance develops strength of character and character strengthens our confident hope of salvation." I was confident that even in a difficult RN program, God would allow me to rejoice and endure. As such, I enrolled and graduated from Louisiana State University with a Bachelor of Science in Nursing.

As my journey continued, I enrolled in a nurse practitioner program at the University of Southern Mississippi. Not only was this program difficult, it was even more complicated because of the amount of reading. As an auditory learner, I remember information when I hear it. If given a text and told what to look for, I'm able to skim and gather the needed information. However, this program required an insurmountable amount of reading. I knew God had led me to this program and the only way I was going to make it was by prayer. I prayed Zechariah 4:6 and asked for the Holy Spirit to lead me. As a result, I met a classmate who told me the only way she could study was by reading and explaining what she learned. Over the course of the program we studied together and I was able to read at my pace and take notes, as she explained what she read. God connected me to my "ram in the bush" and in 2014, I graduated.

If I connect the dots, I'm able to see how every twist in my life had purpose. Through the molestation, I later found my voice to speak up for those patients who are often treated like numbers and not people. I affectionately refer to my patients as *my people*. *My people* are those who have often been frowned upon due to their medical insurance or lack thereof. *My people* are the single, unwed mothers who are desperate to be treated with respect by medical providers. *My people* are the patients who struggle with reading medical recommendations and need some extra help deciphering the paper. *My people* are the teenage girls who've had multiple sexual partners and lack the proper understanding about how to take care of their bodies. *My people* are the disenfranchised population who deserve to be treated with respect, compassion and love.

My journey in the medical field has allowed me to care for patients through managing clinics, serving in labor and delivery and pre-op surgery, and leading nurses as a charge nurse. In 2015, I was a founding member of Black Nurses Rock, Inc. I later became president of the local Mississippi Gulf Coast chapter of Black Nurses Rock.

When people hear the word "trailblazer" it often denotes a monumental achievement. For me, a trailblazer is someone who understands that God first blazes the trail and through His grace He allows us to walk on it. As a 43-year old African American Nurse Practitioner, I am walking the trail God blazed. I've learned that trailblazers don't walk the trail alone. God used people like my grandmother, Mrs. Louise Bowens; my best friend, Mrs. Bianca Lott Bell; and my son's grandmother, Mrs. Barbara Davis, to walk along the trail with me. They supported me when I couldn't support myself. Beyond these women, God even began the healing process between my mother and I. God has applied pressure at different points in my life and that pressure has been my catalyst for achievement. Out of the ashes of a dark childhood came beauty. The fragrance from the ashes still reminds me of the tragedy, but the beauty reminds me of the triumph.

I was once the girl who hated herself. I am now the woman I was waiting for. Always remember, you are the one.

"We are the ones we have been waiting for." – Alice Walker

Walk your blazed trail.

About Kimaka Bowens

Kimaka Bowens is an experienced Nurse Practitioner with a Master's Degree in Nursing Science; focus area Family Nurse Practitioner. She received her degree from the University of Southern Mississippi. Kimaka is no stranger to the healthcare industry having spent over nineteen years in healthcare serving in multiple levels of nursing, beginning at an entry level Medical Assistant expanding to an Advanced Practice Registered Nurse.

Kimaka specializes in Urgent Care, Women's Health, and Weight Loss. In addition to her career in healthcare, Kimaka is also the President of the Non-Profit Nursing Organization, Black Nurses Rock Mississippi Gulf Coast Chapter. Kimaka's varied background in Nursing and Community Service has shaped her to be the caring individual she is today.

Kimaka is passionate about providing quality healthcare to the community and positively impacting all she encounters. She can be reached via email: mskimaka@gmail.com.

LORETTA BRIDGES

Unrecognized Self Worth
Loretta Bridges

God took my ordinary self and transformed me into making a difference in an extraordinary way. The pillar of it all stemmed from me and my sister, Philisa's, upbringing by our stay-at-home mom, Carolyn, and dad, Mack, who could do almost anything with his hands and later become a trucking business entrepreneur. Having been taught the values of honesty, education, and hard work is a blessing that rules my life today. With all that, I was still stuck in low self–esteem, which led to **comfort in stagnation, bad relationship choices, and no satisfaction** all due to a lack of a much-needed spiritual healing and a renewed mind.

God, along with my strong work ethic, brought me out of the attitude of not being good enough and into gratitude of having more than enough. Two of my positive attributes were my belief in God and work ethic. Regardless of what I was going through, my faith in God always made me feel better spiritually, and work did it for me physically. Although, my challenges caused me to struggle to stay positive, I worked harder to feel important instead of doing what was important for others and myself. This mirrored merely surviving to fit in with the world and not living my purpose.

Until one day, I needed a part-time job and became a teller. Yes, I guess handling other people's money made me feel important. Don't judge - I was good at it. Be good at whatever job you hold. Proverb 18:16 states: "A man's gift makes room for him and brings him before great men. I found solace in what I saw as a job to later turn into a career.

Comfort in stagnation began during my work as a casino cashier for 6 years I did not outgrow it quick enough but on time. I worked with a great group of people who remain as good friends, but I grew to know the job was not forever and that God had something more and different for me. A friend and I took the real estate exam, obtained our licenses, and began working as agents. After this, I became a bank teller for four more years (I will explain this later). I attended a Jackson State Football game and a former classmate overheard me tell someone I worked for the bank. I guess I sounded too proud in my statement, because the "ear hustler" responded in a sarcastic way, "do you run the bank or count the money?"

Although, I hid it well, that comment made me feel ridiculously small as if I wasn't important. It is important to note that we should never let others define us. In this case, this one made me feel bad enough to seek better. Always accomplish things in life because it is pleasing to self and God, not people. It was his statement that moved me, soon I no longer felt proud of my job. Self consciously, God allowed that comment to shift my mindset. I used it to self-examine and transform me instead of breaking me.

Bad relationship choices are defined by those I allowed to use me in order to only feel a sense of belonging. Humility, kindness, and low self-esteem could attract the best and the worst people. Mostly the latter, and less of the best. Humility and kindness are obvious attractions to most, mixed with a little lack of confidence is a recipe for attracting the wrong dominant person, or one with the wrong motives. For me, the motives were far from the much needed and deserved love. The takeaway is surrounding we around the right people is one of the keys to your success.

No satisfaction came from the things in which I placed my money, hope, and time before God, this was nothing less than a waste and displeasing to God Not prioritizing was the outcome of no satisfaction. Spending more time doing what I wanted, instead of with God and doing what He wanted. I do believe we should have some of what we want, but not if it means placing those things before God. Happiness is what God wants for us but being granted that happiness is God's provision for us, if we put Him first in all we do.

Being a cashier for six years and a teller for four, as a college graduate, brought both frustration and humbleness to my life. The frustration led me to seeking a better-paying job and the humbleness was the virtue that got me through. My breakthrough had come and finally I had overcome my lack of confidence after taking and passing the real estate exam.

Becoming a real estate agent was liberating, until a life-changing event occurred: a failing marriage had reached its end. Back to being a teller I went, but not for long. The difference this time around is I was content and more grateful to just have a job so I could take care of my three children and pay bills. One day, while referring a customer to do something more to gain a better return on the money on deposit, the market president overheard the conversation and later asked me to apply for a financial service representative position. He saw something in me that I did not see in myself. I later took the state insurance license exam in order to sell annuity and life insurance for the bank

After about four years of doing this, my then branch manager pulled something more out of me and encouraged me to become a branch manager, even in my contentment, this job came to fruition. I wore several hats in this position. I was a commercial and consumer loan officer, market Community Reinvestment Act coordinator, and licensed annuity rep.

As CRA coordinator, I presented financial literacy classes to youth and adults, created relationships with non-profit organizations that serve low- and moderate-income communities, and served on the boards of some of those organizations. Little did I know that this was preparing me for my next job, now career.

After four years in the latter position, a downward spiral. I began facing issues on the job like never. I realized those issues were allowed because something more was brewing. The issues pushed me to the next position in my career as Regional CRA Specialists.

The difference between this position and all others is it was led by my heart's desire and not a financial desire alone, and most of all a desire to give back to the community. Not only was this a lateral move but I also did not know what the increase in pay would be until a later date. I tried to put up a fight, but God said, "GO ANYWAY", God won and in return so did I. Showing my worth was more concrete than kicking and screaming.

I can say this job defines my career in banking. It is incredibly unique in the financial world because it enables me to identify and address the needs of low- and moderate -income communities and fulfill those needs with the help of market leaders and teammates. In all my jobs, I'd never ask anyone to do anything I wouldn't do myself, not just because I'm humble but because I knew how and had no problem doing it when necessary.

In my contentment, I was invited to share this story. Did I consider myself a trailblazer? Not prior to this. This story will hopefully inspire someone who thinks it's not possible to overcome stagnation, bad relationships, no satisfaction, go from an entry level position to a corporate position, and know that it wouldn't have happened without God and the people He places in your path.

So yes, with gratefulness and humility I am the trailblazer who is passionate about serving others, collaborative to get the job done, a little disruptive for the sake of good, and a visionary for the people.

My prayer for and with every woman or man that thinks it's too late to walk in their destiny, renew your mind, and go for it. For those raising children, please encourage and support their dreams from youth to maturity, push them to do the work, don't allow others to define you, and allow God to do the rest through prayer and walking with Him daily.

My personal prayer is that I accomplish all God has planned for me in my service to Him and that my children; Kiaro, Tia, Hosea, and the newest edition, Grandbaby Embri, will continue by doing the same.

I now have a testimony, that would not have been without the test and trials, and contentment in Christ. Because Kearn saw more in me, I also overcame the lack of confidence the enemy tried to destroy me with. I'm finally walking in my destiny after taking the long route. Thanks to Kearn for allowing me to share, and look for more to come from me!

About Loretta Bridges

Loretta is a motivator, financial and life educator, and loves God. Her desire to serve the community proceeds her. Being a resident of the MS Gulf Coast has been the unplanned highlight of her life. She obtained her BS degree in Marketing from Jackson State University in 1992, and her financial career began in 2002 in banking.

Her current location on the Mississippi Gulf Coast enables her to work in several familiar Metropolitan Statistical Areas, including portions of, the Gulf Coast, Mississippi Pine Belt, Alabama and the Florida Panhandle. "Seeking and creating opportunities is my job, and the key to the success of the communities I serve".

Not having a lot of people in her corner, but having the right people helped her to recognize her own value by bringing her out of her struggles with low self-esteem, as God would have it.

DR. MARY KAYE HOLMES

The Struggle Is Real
Dr. Mary Kaye Holmes

I recently heard someone say, "The struggle is NOT real!" Yes, that sounds good and it's very tempting to believe, however, the struggle is not only *very* real, but it's also rewarding. See, my philosophy is this: you have to make the struggle work for you. You simply take every setback, every pitfall, every obstacle, and you own it. Use the adversity to your advantage. Use the pain to produce your purpose. Don't struggle with the struggle.

I often tell my coaching clients the story of the caterpillar growing into a beautiful butterfly. Before undergoing a complete metamorphosis, the caterpillar struggles within the confines of the cocoon. It's a small, constricting space, but it's all the caterpillar has. So, it struggles. It's pushing, it's twisting, it's fiercely fighting to be free. It has wings and has the resemblance of a butterfly, but it's not ready to fly on its own. If someone were to come along and cut the cocoon open, the butterfly would have useless wings because flight would never be in its future.

I've learned that before we can soar, we have to first learn how to struggle. Keep in mind that struggle comes in various forms. In 1999, I moved into my freshman dorm as a pregnant teenager. The father was a pedophile who was 21 years my senior. I was just 15 years old when he first scouted me out. And there I was, 17 and just starting my college career with unrealistic goals of having my child in the spring semester and returning to finish my classes with ease. Not only did I have to take the spring semester off, but I would have to drop to part-time in the fall of the following year. I was completely unaware that the father of my child would not only leave the majority of parenting up to me and my mother, but he would get several other teenaged girls pregnant as well. To my dismay, he also became violent, abusive, and prone to severe mood swings. Fear and intimidation kept me from leaving him and his Dr. Jekyll and Mr. Hyde personality also kept me looking forward to the honeymoon stages we would go through following his unbearable abuse.

In spite of the manipulation, the control, and the violence, I never lost my drive to strive for higher education. The way I saw it, education was my golden ticket out of poverty. It was also a healthy distraction from the trauma I was enduring at home. Unfortunately, my boyfriend did all he could to sabotage my success. After earning enough credits to attend nursing school, I set a date to take the entrance exam, but because I didn't yet have a driver's license, I asked him if he could take me. He not only refused to drive me to the test, but he told me he wouldn't pay for it, either. After managing to save up enough cash to pay for the exam, I secretly mapped out the route to the location. It was almost two hours away, but I studied the train schedule and the bus route to the testing site and made my way there on the day of the exam. A few weeks later, I received a letter in the mail notifying me I had passed the exam and I could attend school to become a Licensed Practical Nurse. The overwhelming joy that flooded my veins was indescribable! In that moment, I saw a glimpse of freedom – something I hadn't seen nor felt in years up to that point. I excitedly put the letter on the front of our fridge, hoping my boyfriend would approve. When he came home that night and saw the letter tacked to the fridge he ripped it off, looked at me, and chuckled, "You're not going". Oh, this struggle was real. But it taught me how to survive.

I felt weak when I couldn't muster the courage to stand up to this abusive man. I felt small and vulnerable when he towered above me with clenched teeth and fists. However, day after day I was strategizing my escape. I was determined to one day experience true freedom and when online degrees were introduced I jumped at the opportunity to get back into school. While my boyfriend was in the streets hustling, I was on my computer churning out one assignment after another. My achievements played an instrumental role in helping me to see my self-worth and beyond the confines of my cocoon. I was struggling toward success. Although I was broken and traumatized, I knew that, just like the butterfly, my wings would one day work.

After seven years of abuse, I escaped that relationship and emerged ready to stand on my own. I pressed my way through college for twenty years and after changing my major several times, I set my sights on becoming a lawyer. From 1999 to 2019, I took one class after another until I earned my associates. Later, I received my bachelors. Finally, I achieved my ultimate educational goal when I was awarded my J.D.

While things got worse before they got better, I took the challenges I endured in life and made my pain into my platform. It's been said when you hit rock bottom it's best to land on your back, because if you can look up you can get up! One day I looked up and realized I had lost everything: my jobs, my children, my freedom, and most of all, hope. I lost my sense of self-worth and my self-respect. I even lost my mind.

Now, as a public speaker, I tell countless men and women that through every loss there's a lesson and after every test there's a testimony. The key is this: don't linger on the losses. Throughout life we will experience countless losses, but when the losses become lessons you will never lose again. When I experience a setback, I know it's only a matter of time before I'll come back stronger. I make sure I leave every level with a valuable lesson. If I don't learn the lesson then I'm doomed to repeat the last level. I was tired of regressing. I needed some forward momentum, but moving forward meant I had to learn how to live on my own. I had to learn how to survive without the safety net of my ex-boyfriend. He was controlling and abusive, but he was also the breadwinner. When I left, I had to learn some hard lessons: I was on my own. It was time to fly.

After being confined to a cocoon for so long I imagine the world can look overwhelming to the butterfly. While it's experienced life outside of the cocoon in its prior existence, that life was experienced at its lowest. It had to crawl and could not experience life off the ground. I had to experience life beyond abuse. I had to come out from under the darkness of trauma, learn to breathe on my own, and spread my wings.

Maya Angelou said it best, "People marvel at the beauty of the butterfly, but rarely admit to the changes it has gone through to achieve that beauty."

About Dr. Mary Kaye Holmes

Dr. Mary Kaye Holmes is a corporate lawyer, U.N. Ambassador, #1 International Best-Selling Author, public speaker, and transformation coach. She is also a sought-after, trusted authority on life after trauma. She has been endorsed by Valerie Jarrett, former Senior Advisor to President Obama; Connecticut State Senator Marilyn Moore; and many others.

Dr. Mary is the award-winning CEO of Waterbury Community Action Network, a non-profit dedicated to the underprivileged and underserved. She was awarded an honorary Doctor of Philosophy for her extensive humanitarian contributions and the Mid-Atlantic Region Public Interest Award for leveraging her law career to further her commitment to community. In 2019, she received her U.N. Ambassadorship, with a focus on human-trafficking prevention. In 2020, she joined the Dignity for Incarcerated Women Advisory Board for #Cut50, a criminal justice reform organization under the leadership of CNN's Van Jones.

Dr. Mary currently resides in New York with her supportive husband.

MAVIS A. CREAGH

Triumph over Tragedy

Mavis A. Creagh

My journey is unique to me and my life situations are all my own. One of my biggest struggles was learning to accept myself. Having those difficult conversations that allow true growth and the courage to stand in my truth has been life-altering.

Everyone has a story; some just divulge, depending on their passion and purpose. Sharing before you are healed can be more traumatic, because not everyone will support you.

I would like to share some of my testimony. What was meant to break me allowed me to blossom into the person I am today. Even though it has not been easy, I am grateful for my experiences and struggles along the way.

"Triumph over Tragedy"- Praise the Most High

What may seem like a setback could be the Creator orchestrating an opportunity for ministry. It took me a long time to fully accept my life. It's easy to sugarcoat and gloss over hurt and pain, however, this doesn't help you or anyone else. Share as you are led and be thankful you made it out of the "Pit". If you are still standing after tragedy know there were many who didn't make it out with their mind, spirit, and body. Do not take it lightly and remember not everyone could have carried your burden or endured your cross.

I have never had a fairy tale story. No prince charming, no master's degree in 5 Years, no size 8 pants after childbirth...Yeah, *Not Me*. My story is filled with struggle, jacked-up decisions, and even worse situations. My disposition for the most part was always positive with my catchphrase of ***"It will work out!"*** I had an unshakable faith that did not waiver and looked the world in the face, even when it spit in mine. But this changed over the last few years. The woman who would make lemonade out of dirt became uneasy and afraid. My spirit of expectation, hope, and crazy faith diminished and morphed into doubt and despair. People who I usually encouraged turned around and encouraged me. My positive stance became sarcastic and impatient, leading to unproductivity and no peace.

What would lead me to such a place? I allowed my circumstances to take over my **Being.**

Never allow anyone or anything to overshadow you as a person. You were not created to be a Wife, Mother, Lover, Daughter, Boss, or Employee! You were created to serve the Most High and fulfill your purpose. Although these are noble titles, they do not define you as a **Woman**. When we allow situations and people to overshadow who we are this can open doorways to tragic situations.

One day, I woke up and even joked…*God, it's me, Mavis.* Imagining my angels were probably tired and laughing, thinking they probably needed to stay in shape.

The portion of my journey I will focus on today is self-love. To be at a place where I allowed situations and people to cause me to question my worth, value, and dignity is mind-blowing. At this phase of my life, it appears unimaginable - but not long ago it was tolerated. That's why I never say what will never happen to me, because judging people is the quickest way to be embarrassed by life.

I'm a domestic and sexual abuse survivor. In one previous relationship, I was not the woman who said *enough is enough*. I stayed and endured multiple forms of abuse. After having sustained so much I left only after being forced out. I packed my son and I's belongings in my truck and made exhausting trips for days trying to move all our things out before my ex made it back home. I couldn't see it then, but it was a blessing in disguise. My son was getting older and had never seen me being physically abused, but he was concerned about my wellbeing.

The abuse did not end when we moved. After some tough decisions, I made the conscious choice to cut off all communication and not look back. I was very afraid in the beginning and would hold my breath when my ex tried to reinsert himself in our lives. Over time, I became stronger and knew the Lord would protect and provide. I had to start back over and I remember feeling so proud when I purchased my son his bedroom suite. He went in the store and picked out whatever he wanted. That was my promise to him. I struggled to pay it off, but we were home and we were safe. It wasn't easy, but with faith and perseverance we are doing better now than ever.

It saddens me to see anyone mistreated. Please know you are valuable and beautiful. The Creator does not create junk and you deserve the best that Yeshua (Jesus) has to offer. I hope my testimony helps someone to be set free. Everything that tried to break me made me stronger and wiser.

Selah,

Mavis A. Creagh

Glimpse at the Past

Being a single parent, businesswoman, domestic abuse survivor, and mother of an amazing young man is all worth it. I found an old McAlister's Deli hat from when I worked there a little over 11 years ago right before I moved back to my home of Hattiesburg, Mississippi. I had two jobs, worked overnight at a State Hospital and worked during the day as a cashier and server. Many times, not sleeping for up to 3 days. No transportation, public housing, sometimes having to walk down a highway from work before day, but God! This was with a college degree and I had applied to over 50 jobs.... I was reminded that it doesn't matter where you start but how you handle the journey. I'm not finished so I am yet pressing and trusting the Most High for favor, grace, and provision. The best is yet to come. So, stay in the race!!! Thankful for my journey and all those who remain True Blue!

#Faithful in All Seasons #Way Maker #Faith without Limits

Stepping into My Future

Currently I serve as the Executive Director of R3SM, Inc. (Recover, Rebuild, Restore Southeast MS) in Hattiesburg, MS. Almost 12 years ago following Hurricane Katrina I started out as a case manager through a pilot program that was only supposed to last **6 Months**! R3SM (Recover, Rebuild, Restore Southeast Mississippi) coordinates restoration, rebuilding and disaster recovery services to low-income families and individuals living in Mississippi's Pinebelt. R3SM, Inc. now covers South MS and assists with long term recovery following disasters as well as other community needs such as Affordable Housing, Workforce Development and Training.

Since 2006, R3SM, Inc. has generated almost **$ 23 million**: Almost **$12 million** in grants and private donations; and over **$11 million** in volunteer labor which completed homes, rebuilds, and fully renovated the 10,000 sq. ft. Historic Volunteer House which can house 60 volunteers. The Volunteer House formally known as the "Robinson Inn" is completely owned by R3SM, Inc. Over 600 homes have been renovated through our programs and 40+ New Constructions. R3SM was recently featured by Mississippi Business Journal as one of the top non-profit organizations in the state out of over 20,000!

Currently I have completed my first book, a Women's Devotional that allows others to learn from my personal journey. I am actively involved with various volunteer organizations and serve on multiple State and Regional Boards. Also, a member of the Women's Business Owners of the Pine Belt and recently received their coveted Lifetime Membership Award and have been recognized with a Lifetime Achievement Award. One of my main goals is to empower people who are often overlooked. My passion is to help those in need and strive daily to be of assistance while serving others.

Recently I started a ministry to help women and families, *We Women Ministries,* to promote the development and progression of Women Internationally. *We Women Ministries* assists by being an advocate and provides resources for Women of all ethnicities and cultures. The Deepest Belief is that all Women should be Given a Voice and Deserve to Be Respected. Because Although WE Are Different, WE EMBODY the Spirit of *1*… **We WOMEN**!!! In addition, I am an independent beauty consultant with Mary Kay.

I am a proud graduate of Mississippi State University and majored in Psychology. My greatest gift is being a mother to my teenage son, Jordan. **Jordan literally saved my Life!** In my spare time I enjoy reading, exercising, cooking, writing, gardening, and encouraging others.

About Mavis A. Creagh

Mavis A. Creagh is an advocate, survivor, inspirational leader, motivational speaker, mentor, entrepreneur, and author!

She currently serves as the Executive Director of R3SM, Inc. (Recover, Rebuild, Restore Southeast MS) in Hattiesburg, MS. R3SM, Inc. covers South MS and assists with long term recovery following disasters as well as other community needs.

Her first book; a Women's Devotional, allows others to learn from her personal journey. She assists with various volunteer organizations and serves on multiple boards. Her passion is to help those in need and strives daily to be of assistance while serving others.

Recently she started a ministry to help women and families, *We Women Ministries.*

Mavis is a graduate of Mississippi State University and majored in Psychology. She is the proud mother of a teenage son, Jordan and they reside in Hattiesburg, MS. In her spare time, she enjoys reading, exercising, cooking, writing, gardening, and encouraging others.

OBIOMA MARTIN

Leading Is A Choice
Obioma Martin

It takes courage to continue and be a trailblazer. Often, it's not about success or failure, it's about our "why", which is in alignment with every fiber in our being and causes us to get up and create a path that has never been created before. It's the courage and the "Why", the alignment of the two, that says, I may have made a mistake. I may have failed at this, but I'm going to continue to lean in, I'm going to continue to move forward. I'm going to continue to stand up. I'm going to continue to show up and to show I'm going to continue to press play, because I'm not a failure. I may have failed at this test, but I'm not a failure.

So for me, being a trailblazer - specifically a trailblazer in my community, in my family, and in my industry - is being able to do something that's never been done before. In what was rooted, there was a challenge and there are many challenges we face. But you have to be bold, courageous and fearless enough to say, let me be the one, let me be the answer.

Often, many people are onlookers. Many people are passive buyers, in that they will see a situation and say, wow, I wish somebody did something! Or else they're waiting for somebody else to show up and they miss the opportunity of being an answer, they miss the opportunity of being the person that writes the check, being the one that says, I'll do it, being the one that's going to be the voice for the voiceless.

And so, I often think about my journey as an entrepreneur, but also my journey - specifically in early childhood education, industry, and my journey as an advocate and a mother - and just having this relentless attitude that says, No, I'm going to do this, I'm going to move forward. And so it takes me back to a situation or challenge, where the community you have is four people iand you have children who are in need of quality early education. You have single moms, married women, women who are broken, women who are depleted, women who are unemployable, women who lack skills, knowledge and education, but yet they still have to feed their family.

You also have women who have just surrendered to what life has dealt them, and so they find themselves in a situation where they're now dependent on assistance from society, from the welfare program, or from a workforce development program. And then you have the welfare system the social service designed to help, but it really doesn't help, it's just a crutch because when said individuals actually go to the system for help, as soon as they come up just a little bit, their benefits begin to get cut off and they find themselves being stuck all over again, because how is it they're able to feed their family off minimum wage. And so, they're not making enough to feed their family but yet they cut their food stamps off and say they want these mothers to work, to go to school, but yet they cut childcare support off. And so these individuals find themselves stuck.

Then you have the Workforce Development Program that sees the opportunity to get paid off, individuals are a resource by being the answer, but there are still gaps in this system. And so for me, I saw the challenge and I made a choice to be the answer. I was able to create a trail and blaze through, because I've decided to do something that hadn't been done before. I created a pipeline, if you will, or early childhood work for a Workforce Development program that was service, the challenges of all four people.

What will happen now is the child would receive continuity and quality of service, the mom would then receive training and her benefits will stay because she's in a qualified activity that will allow her to continue to receive food stamps and cash and medical support - whatever it is she needs in terms of sustainability, the Welfare to Work Program, or the welfare system. They're now winning because they're providing a service to the person who needed it. Then the Workforce Development Program, of course, is helping this individual with resources so they can be employable and obtain education.

So I decided to use some elements, systems, and resources that already existed and bring them together and then served them to all four individuals. My choice was then that I'm going to teach this program that supply the resources or the tools to all four people. What I needed to do was just say, Yes, really. I already have the knowledge, the education, and the resources, and it was just a matter of me saying "yes" and that's really what a trailblazer does. They just simply say yes, I'll be the one. I'll be the one, you can pick me, I'll be the mouthpiece, the voice, I'll do the heavy lifting.

It reminds me of the story of the border in the Bible, where God was trying to raise men up and say, listen, I need you to go out and conquer this land, but the king at that time was like, Nah, I'm not going anywhere but the border. If you go I'll go with you.

And so women who were raised in divorce ended up being the Trailblazers in this story, because they said, you know what, I'm going to go but if I go women are going to get the credit. That was unheard of, because the bar was the judge at the time and so she said, Okay, let's do this. And so the story continues in jL, who was just a woman who also was a trailblazer, but she was also courageous and fearless when Brock, the enemy, came into her camp. She seductively laid him down gave him something to drink and created a safe place for him. Then she took a nail and nailed it into his temple and killed him. Surely the women got the credit, because we were willing to do what man was unwilling to. Again, that is who a trailblazer is, and that is what a true blazer does.

About Obioma Martin

Obioma Martin is an international transformational speaker, B.R.E.A.T.H.E. accountability-coach, author, small business expert, childcare strategist and esteemed advocate for women's empowerment. Martin's passion for equipping women with the tools they need to, not only survive but, prosper and live audaciously, has launched her into a life of unparalleled servitude, wherein she continues to thrive by helping others.

Martin has helped over 5000 women get off welfare and get the credentials required to complete and further their education. A life-long learner herself, Martin holds multiple degrees; associates in Early Childhood Education, Bachelor's in Childcare Management, a master's degree in Early Childhood Education and Leadership, Goldman Sachs 10,000 Small Business Program alumni, certified biblical counselor, and ordained evangelist.

Contact Martin at obioma@obiomamartin.com

Follow her on FB@obiomamartin.com, IG@iamobiomamartin.com

Website www.omazingyou.com

PAULA JOHNSON - HUTCHINSON

How Interdependence Created Second to None
Paula Johnson - Hutchinson

I am often asked how in the world did I come up with the name Second to None for my brand. The name alone has put me in rooms that I did not belong in. What the name means to me now versus when I started out is a totally different meaning. So, I am going to share why this name means so much to me for the first time within this platform. I feel like it is the right time to reminisce on the past, enjoy the present, and declare the future of Second to None.

In my younger days, I often said that my business name derived from a rap group at the time. I was 25 and there was a group from the West coast with the name. I loved it! But when I really think about the name, I know in my heart that it came from a deeper place. It came from a hurt that I experienced early on as an entrepreneur. I was working in a well- known salon in my area. I knew from day one of cosmetology school, that I wanted my own salon. I even stated it aloud on my first day of school when our teacher asked our class what we wanted to be at the time. I did not know it then, but I was already making a declaration of what my future would look like.

Back to my statement about working in a well-known salon at the time. It had gotten back to me that one of my beloved mentors in the industry made a statement that "I had good ideas but lacked follow through." I was offended beyond degree. I realized in that moment that my mentor did not value me. She did not value my growth as a stylist up to that point. She did not value who I was at that time. When she first met me, I was rough around the edges. By the time this statement was made, I was married and pregnant with my second child. As a young woman, I felt let down and targeted because the person she told it to was a man. Now she did apologize and maybe it was some immaturity on her part. Maybe I was still showing some signs of roughness. What I did know is that I was better than she assumed. That moment sparked a fire in me. I came home and cut on the television with rap videos displayed all over the screen. Low and behold here comes a video with the beforementioned group. Second to None became not only the name of my business but the beginning of a lifestyle for me.

About six months after this incident and confrontation, I got blessed with my own salon. I had been an entrepreneur by being a booth renter but now, I had bills. I also had to build a name. And what was that name? You already know that it was Second to None. I started promoting and my salon quickly gained a buzz. I began working long hours, traveled as an educator and then grew from 600 square feet to a salon that was 1400 square feet. I then opened a spa location and a salon with 22 chairs. I went from "this little salon" as some people called it to a well-respected figure in my industry. I was also blessed to sit on boards and panels for businesses. Soon, the name Second to None was all over my area.

Then, my husband took a job out of town just as our last child graduated. I was on this huge career high and agreed to move over 1000 miles away. This story may be long or even seem like it's dragging but I am going somewhere with this. Once I moved, I was still going back and forth working, slowly transitioning my business from Louisiana to Arizona. Finally, I closed my business in my hometown and began the path of creating my business in Arizona. This meant identifying a space, building clientele and making a profit. In my mind, I had been at this point before. Now this is where the story is going to get good.

When I first opened, I had 3 clients in one month. That is not a misprint. I really had only 3 clients. Keep in mind that I am used to having my book filled without openings on a consistent basis. This average did not happen just one month, it continued to happen. Once I got to month number 9, I was mentally defeated. I had the nerve to be in school pursuing a degree in business, over economic and development committees, and was awaiting approval to be a mentor with a national organization…with no clients. I was outdone to say the least and an ager grew up in me that I had never experienced, so I thought. Just when That was going on, my health started to take a turn towards needing surgery. This meant any plans I had created to change the trajectory of my business were going to be put on hold. I was in a depression and disbelief that was immeasurable. I had been so used to being successful, driven and happy, I forgot that drought seasons are also a part of the entrepreneurial process. I was not prepared.

But during my healing time and hidden depression, God reminded me of Second to None. He caused me to have dreams of when I first started my business. He caused me to remember how I got to be successful in my industry. I collected myself, scratched my old plan and began to rebuild. If you are wondering, here comes the lesson in it all.

When you make the decision to go after your dreams, they can take you anywhere. You never know how your vision will manifest itself and take on a life of its own. What you also can never discount is the power of interdependence. See, interdependence means relying on others and them relying on you. In other words, it does take a village. What I finally realized that my revamped plans had me working on my own and not with others. The community helped me to build my business in the past, but somewhere along the way, I omitted needing community to build in a new place. Once I recovered from surgery, I immediately started networking in my new community. I began meeting people that needed my services and I began to provide the exceptional service that is Second to None. I began vending my own hair care products again along with shipping to my former clients back home. See, I didn't realize that my business was not in a season of decline but a season of expansion! When you do not recognize the signs of your season, especially in entrepreneurship, you can grow to hate what you love. You can develop community-deaf ears and start thinking you don't belong in the room with success. Negative perspective coming from within the person that created the brand will kill a business faster than any critics on the outside of the brand. I had to humble myself and return to my roots. I had to treat my business like a re-potted plant. My business was not dead, it was just shocked for a second. Had I continued the neglect of my brand; I would have lost everything that I worked for.

Fast forward to today, I have expanded my salon in a new area, on boards for business, part of national entrepreneurship organizations, and in this book! You must align your thoughts on what you want to see. You cannot disconnect to support sources and continued education for your business. You must fight when nobody else will. You cry, get organized and go at it again. You must have others to lean on. You do not know everything. You must depend on your community and trust them to grow you. You need the interdependence to hold you up when you cannot stand on your own. In entrepreneurship, you must not lose connectivity to lifelines. My name means so much more now because it is winning me awards in my new area and putting me before larger groups than ever before. At age 46, I can honestly say that the Second to None name was God given and drew community around me. I am a living testimony that even in your darkest times, there is light and light. Second to None means a lifestyle to me. I am good at what I do, and I used my brand name to motivate me in every move that I make. Without my community, my name would have no value. Whatever industry you are in, if you remember none of what I wrote, remember the word interdependence.

About Paula Johnson - Hutchinson

Paula Johnson Hutchinson is a beauty entrepreneur and business consultant. As the owner of Second to None Hair Salon and Second to None Hair Care Systems, she has been able to create an award-winning career path. As the owner of PH Factor Consulting Firm, she works to help entrepreneurs identify their niche and develop strategic implementation plans. She creates safe space events for women called Stiletto Talks across the country, a SCORE Mentor and currently serves as the City Director of Phoenix for Walker's Legacy, which is a nationally recognized entrepreneur platform for women of color. She holds certifications as a cosmetologist, cosmetology educator and has a B.S. degree in Business from University of Phoenix.

SABRINA STALLWORTH

Genie In A Bottle
Sabrina Stallworth

The journey of life has its twists and turns it is important for us to embrace every challenge because it is part of getting to the next level. Sometimes we may not understand the path, but we must embrace the journey. After, I lost my job with Delta Airlines I became depressed and started drinking heavily. I would drink a fifth of Tequila in two days and a gallon in three that was my way of dealing with loss and shame. I was devastated about losing my fifteen year career with Delta Airlines the career that allowed me the luxury of traveling the world-Europe, Mexico, Aruba, Jamaica, all over the US. I built my home from the ground up, purchased a new sports car, I had five platinum ,and it was all gone with the blink of an eye. I was in management and responsible for other people it was so embarrassing a two day weekend trip of balling out in New Orleans, would change my life forever. The devastation was very traumatic for me I worked so hard and now it was gone. I remember going through a very dark stage of depression. My mom and best friend (Tonya) would call me everyday, they were concerned with my mental state, I assured them I was okay and not suicidal. One day I was standing in my kitchen washing dishes gazing into my backyard and I began to break down, and cry. I was depressed and unsure of how I was going to maintain my finances then I heard a voice say "I will never forsake you". I immediately stopped crying and began to pray through all the pain I knew the Divine Creator had my back. There was an urgency for me to clear my mind and get a sense of my life back. I felt the quote by Andy in the movie Shawshank Redemption "Get busy living or get busy dying" I was tired of dying and wanted to live again. My mother(Joyce), and I made earrings years ago, and she suggested that I get back into being creative so, I took her advice, and started crafting I made earrings and a bible marker at the request of a friend. I grabbed a bottle of Tequila to pour myself a drink and a vision came over me of that bottle of Tequila so creative nothing like I have experienced before. I started putting wires, and beads on the bottles creating decorative bottle decanters; they were beautiful ornamental displays. I began having dreams that the bottles had arms and legs, so I taught myself how to drill holes in the bottles, and use wire for the arms, and legs eventually what was once a bottle was transforming into a figurative piece of artwork . What was occurring was above my own comprehension.

God was directing my vision to see beyond the liquor, but to see the possibilities of what that bottle could be. I was using drinking as an outlet, God was showing me my destiny. I would have dreams during the day time and I would rush home and figure out how to create it. My friend encouraged me to build a business God gave me the name not knowing this vision would be the beginning stages of the birthing of "AllBottledUpByBre". I was working with bottles and what was about to be birthed was all bottled up in me. Next, there was nothing out there like what I was doing so it was a learning curve. I started creating women like people I would make them clothes and dress them up. I started going to thrift stores to purchase leather, and suede pieces. I would take the items I purchased apart, and clean them. Everybody loved my art and work people would commission me to do things. I would go to Tandy Leather stores and buy hides, and exotic skins. When people saw my art they thought it was clay but it was just a bottle people would ask me "How did you do that" creating art let to people asking me to make purses, handbags, and shoes. I taught myself through tutorials and books everything was always taught because I didn't have the money. Through my depression and emptiness the Divine Creator was revealing to me that the bottle had something far more valuable than the Tequila. A deep purpose and passion was unfolding right before me that voice "I will never forsake you" showed up in a bottle and changed the dynamics of my life.

Lastly, today I am a Executive Board of Trustee at the Ohr-O' Keefe museum of Art. I am apart of two art associations and facilitate jewelry making classes. My ultimate vision is to open my own Art Gallery to sell other creative artist artwork, and to teach leather, and jewelry making to other people who might be going through dark times. A trailblazer is someone who can see beyond what is in front of them someone who can be instrumental in encouraging others to see their potential. I have learned on my journey the Divine Creator of life has your back all you need to do is pray, ask for guidance and discernment in everything you do. When we put our trust in the Divine Creator everything will be revealed and manifest in our favor. My desire in life is to be of service to others in extracting the creativity they possess when they find themselves in a deep hole of depression, for we are all divinely created to create.

About Sabrina Stallworth

Sabrina Stallworth was born in Biloxi, Mississippi,but she grew up in Atlanta, Georgia, she attended college in Savannah, Georgia and lived on the island of Oahu, Hawaii. These cities she called home have influenced her distinctive style.

Sabrina, or (Bre), as her friends call her, is a self-taught artisan her unique leather accessories,and art creations have been exhibited with The National Arts Program in Fulton County, Georgia, The Peter Anderson Arts Festival, ArtsAlive Arts Festival, Success Women's Conference,and NOLA Fashion Week.

Sabrina,is a active Ohr-O'Keefe Museum of Art Board of Trustee member,and a member of local Arts associations.

Her creations are available for purchase at The Ohr-O'Keefe Museum of Art,speciality boutiques,and commissioned work.

When Bre is not creating she enjoys teaching others her craft. Book her for your private or group class today.

SANDY SANDERS

Time and Words

Sandy Sanders

As I think of time oh wow do I see the reel–to-reel image of my life spinning like that of an old classroom projector full of color, unlike the black and white images in the 60's, full of scenes and episodes leading to this moment. The moment in which I now can tell the young girl Sandy, "you got through it." It is my hope that by the time you read this you, too, will be able to help the young version of yourself break free and live as authentic as you can.

As a young girl I was told I would never amount to anything by the very people in my life who were meant to give positive words and correct me. For the record, I will say my momma raised me well, took me to church, community activities, and made sure I looked good and acted proper. Back in the day we called it "walking the straight and narrow". However, those times when I messed up bad is when they'd be tearing down with words of negativity, "you not gon be this" "you not gon be that." That's all I remembered - words my momma chose to use as well as the words I chose to remember. Sounds like selective hearing to me! I'm sure she just wanted me to "be somebody" as she would call it a place of respect in the community, just as she had earned. So I don't blame her, I just wish she had used a better choice of words.

Words can shape one's life for sure. I had low self-esteem and always felt I was never good enough. I made bad choices in almost every area of my younger life, and it's because I believe it was the younger version of myself who was navigating my actions. I had no care of the consequences, therefore I continued throughout my teen years searching for love with the wrong individuals and the things that came along with them.

Love, the first word I had no clue what IT looked like or felt like, because it was not heard at all that I can remember. Little girls should hear they are loved by their father and mother - those that care for them. I've had to go back and even now today to tell the young Sandy, "I know you were hurt but **I do love you**" and "**it's okay to love**". The scripture God is Love

129

1 John 4:8 helped me know and learn that God made me, created me, He knows all about me and all through my bad experiences and wrong choices, Jesus's love kept me ALIVE, literally. When I was depressed and didn't know how to articulate it, when I would drink so I would not feel the pain, or fall in the arms of a man who would continue to abuse me. Oh it was God's love that mended, restored and held me together through brokenness and disappointments in myself - not what others did to me, but what *I* did to me. The words "I am Sorry", " I am Forgiven", "I Forgive", became seeds of God's Word and caused me to grow and become who I am today.

Philippians 1:6 became the fertilizer, if you will, it says in the Amplified Version: *I am convinced and confident of this very thing, that He who has begun a good work in you will [continue to] perfect and complete it until the day of Christ Jesus [the time of His return].* So, every time the personality or character of the young Sandy would show up with feelings of doubt, insecurity, and uncertainty, I would pull out my bible and read that scripture.

Overcomer, to get the better of in a struggle or conflict; conquer; defeat; to overcome the enemy; to prevail over (opposition, a debility, temptations, etc.) that comes to mind because I had to overcome the years of negative words spoken to me as a child. Giving birth to the most amazing three children, who have help me become an overcomer. They stuck by me during those dark days, beginning when I   was an unwed mother (that's what they called it back then) at 20 years old to my oldest daughter and I certainly had to overcome some things because I didn't know how to be a mom mentally - I was still a child myself in my mind and spirit.

As I was trying to find peace within myself of my past one day, I sat down and thought back to the young 20-year-old inner girl in me and this is what I told her: "the little baby you were so afraid to love, well that baby grew up, she is 38 years old and now through years of difficultly a mother and daughter relationship has matured into a great place. God saw how you both needed each other in many ways, well He has restored your relationship because you prayed and was open to accept those things you couldn't change and to change those things that could. Oh how we've

OVERCOME so much." Having that flashback was a major breakthrough. So if you're struggling with things in your past, like mistakes or hurt, I encourage you to go back to that little girl in you and ask God to help you to forgive and let go. It's then you can walk in the fullness of who you are, free and with the spirit of forgiveness.

Forgiveness, the action or process of forgiving or being forgiven. I had to forgive myself, but most of all I had to forgive others and ask others to forgive me. Psychologists generally define forgiveness as a conscious, deliberate decision to release feelings of resentment or vengeance toward a person or group who has harmed you, regardless of whether they actually deserve your forgiveness. Forgiveness does not mean forgetting, nor does it mean condoning or excusing offenses. I will be the first to admit it's not easy for some to forgive, but because I've had to forgive both myself and others, I'll say it's certainly possible. I try to share that hope of forgiveness with my children. However, it's only possible through our Lord Jesus Christ, not through our own power. Jesus gave me the ability to forgive, it was done through much prayer and applying and studying His Forgiveness brings much freedom, it's like letting go of that dirty blanket you carry around on your shoulder - you remember the Charlie Brown character Linus and that blanket he always had? Well, that's what our "unforgiveness" is like. It becomes the security one sometimes holds onto and then it becomes something that's holding you back. You must let go and forgive so that you're free in both your mind, body and soul. Something I've often shared with the women I teach at our local jail who are incarcerated during our Life Skills Classes is that forgiveness is the first key to your freedom.

Obedience is compliance with an order, request, law or submission to another's authority. We don't talk about that word much, but it's an ingredient God uses to shape my life. Being disobedient can bring consciences that can alter one's life dramatically. For example, not eating correctly, I would find it easier to grab fast food rather than cooking, which resulted in high cholesterol. Or smoking, that nasty smelling habit that gets on your clothes, hair, pores - you name it. I was a "closet smoker", I did it in the privacy of my home until I found myself unconvincing my husband and children constantly going to the hospital because I couldn't breathe.

131

Finally, after so many emergency visits to the hospital and feeling I was going to die, I finally quit and God restored my lungs. After all my disobedience and rebelliousness, God's love toward me healed me. Now on Sundays, every now and then you will find me taking a victory lap around the church praising God.

I recognized it's better to be obedient than to suffer the consequences of being disobedient. Conveying that to women who are incarcerated is oh so real. I was called to Jail Ministry while teaching my class to the women and I began to share my testimony. In my sharing it was like a light bulb came on - I realized that I too could have been sitting right there, behind locked doors, incarcerated, locked up. I struggled with a drinking habit many years ago, where I would drink every day, get up the next morning, get dressed, go to a corporate job, come home and do it all over again. One night after going out to the club, I left the bar as a drunk driver. I'm not sure how I made it home, but God kept me from killing myself or someone else. It's obvious I had a bad hangover the next day, but fast forward and here I am telling this story to incarcerated females who were also suffering the consequences of their actions or their addiction. I stood telling them and that's when I knew I could tell them of the love of Jesus Christ and how he saved me, spared my life and someone else's life. I remember the eyes of those women as I shared my story, how I became vulnerable and transparent about the saving Grace of my Savior. It displayed his sovereign love and spared me the consequences of my actions. That day I felt a level of freedom I hadn't known before. Many will find themselves saying, "why do you want to help someone who is locked up and in jail?" and my answer would be, "Jesus will show up in the jail". I pray with and teach many women who are incarcerated and also mentor them when they're released.

Remember words have power and I end with proverb 15:4 "Gentle **words** bring life and health; a deceitful tongue crushes the spirit." Proverbs 16:24 "Kind **words** are like honey–sweet to the soul and healthy for the body." Proverb 18:4 "A person's **words** can be life-giving water; **words** of true wisdom are as refreshing as a bubbling brook."

Sandy Sanders

About Sandy Sanders

Sandy Sanders, an author and Social Media Show Host, a talking segment and conversation of topics that are encouraging, inspiring and uplifting. Her 25+ years of experience as a Contact Center Specialist and Manager, prepared her also to train and teach life skill classes to female inmates in the local Adult Detention Center. She is qualified from her experience and certifications to train church congregations that are interested in starting a Jail Ministry. Sandy services as an active Board member of Transition Inc. a nonprofit organization that provides housing for women recently released. She is a Licensed Evangelist where she serves in various capacities in her local church. Sandy is a wife, mother of 3 Adult children and grandmother. She co-authored the Anthology Notes to Younger Women and her recent publication Gratitude Journal 2020 . Sandy is available for speaking engagements and workshop training.

Website : www.coffeeconversationswithsandy.com /email coffeeconversationwithsandy@gmail.com

SHAWN LARE' BRINKLEY

My Coming Out Party
Shawn LaRe' Brinkley

Michelle Obama stated in an interview with Oprah on her 2020 Visionaries Tour, "It's time to own our stories!" That resonates with me. So many of us want to hide our stories. We want to hide behind a mask of deceit! Now, I'm not calling anyone a liar, but when you cover up your truth then life itself becomes a lie. My offering, as I tell a part of my story, is that we all come out from behind our masks and stand boldly in the truth of our "Who-We-Are-Ness!"

I like to make up words, so I'll explain. Your "Who-You-Are-Ness" represents your authentic self...the innermost parts of you. The parts of you that God knit together when you were in the womb, just like in Psalm 139. Many of us run from that part of ourselves, perhaps because we fear the unknown! I too have hidden behind the facade of who I thought I should be! Let me tell you how I came out.

As a child growing up in Toledo, Ohio, my parents didn't thwart my burgeoning personality. Though they didn't spare the rod when I was off on one of my adventures gone bad, they always allowed me to exercise my creativity. I was the kid who would tell all the others in the classroom, "drop your notebooks when the clock strikes twelve", or "when the bell rings, everyone throw the balls on the top of the building." As a result of these little episodes, the teachers had my parents on speed dial. One time, they said to my Daddy, "Mr. Williams, we believe Shawn is a leader, however, we have some concerns as to which direction she will lead the children." I'm sure part of the issue was ADHD, but I was a '60s baby, so no one was talking about that, especially in the black community. Instead they said, "Woo, that baby got a lot of energy." Grandma Johnson said, "That baby move like 90 goin' north." I now use it as my superpower.

Well, I managed to graduate high school and off I went to college. I started out at Ohio University in Athens and after a year there, I managed to convince my parents I needed greater academic challenges and transferred to New York University. Completely excited, I arrived in New

York City, but little did I know that life was about to change. I made it out of New York University unscathed, but shortly thereafter life would offer lemons from which I would find it ever so challenging to make lemonade. On my way to work to teach dance to elementary school children, I got out of a taxi, but the driver took off, dragging me approximately two and a half feet and the back wheel ran over the calf of my leg. I suffered severe back, leg, and neck injuries.

Now, this was the first of a three-part drama that became my life. I was in a second taxi accident, where the taxi was hit from behind by a truck, knocking us into a pole in front of my favorite restaurant. Subsequently, the last of this accidental triplicate began with me crossing the street in Harlem, after getting my hair braided and getting hit by a produce truck turning left into me. Here is where I began to learn the meaning of the word *resilience*. I was told I would never dance again, I had short-term memory loss, chronic pain, and I gained 100 pounds in a year and a half; after having been a beauty queen four times over.

I went from my bathing-suit bared body to my sweat-suit covered body. I didn't know what to do with the pain I was living; physical, mental, and emotional pain seared through me, changing who I was. Absent from the fullness of who I was, I became present with the me who used food as source of relief; a tool to mask the truth of my pain. I didn't know how to grieve my life while still living it. So, I faked it. I pretended to be fine, well, good with the chubby, happy lady. I laughed and became known as the "full figured Diva". I modeled in fashion shows for Pretty Hot and Thick Girls (PHAT). As I strutted my stuff in designer finery, tossing my hair, and swiveling my ample hips, I secretly longed to be a size 10 as I had been when the taxi driver disrupted my flow and pressed his all too eager pedal to the metal, altering my life as I knew it.

While I was recovering from each of those "incidents" I endured, I really didn't know how to not be the happy girl, for that is who I was naturally. I didn't know what to do with feelings of loss, fear, anger, or hurt I was experiencing from this drastic shift in my life. I had to learn it was okay for me to be down sometimes, to not feel great, to own my true feelings, to be sad. I didn't know what this looked like. I had never given myself permission to be sad. When I had previously experienced difficulty, I hadn't faced my true feelings. Each day is a lesson and a blessing. I know this so well, as I had to gather strength to get up every day in pain and find the reason to "do it all over again."

Believe it or not, there are silver linings attached to this story, the greatest of which is I am alive to share this with you. The most valuable take away from this trilogy of tragedy is I learned God had a purpose for my life, which I had to discover and become aligned. I began to understand in a first-hand and real kind of way that tomorrow is not promised to anyone and when you're given a second and a third chance, you must find your greatness. In my quest to find my greatness, I realized it was never lost. You see, sometimes we search for what makes us great by looking outside ourselves when indeed the "thing" that lives inside you that makes you *you* is where your greatness resides. Your greatness is in your acceptance of who you are and learning to love that person.

Since that essential lesson, I've had some challenges that might knock your socks clear across the room. But now when I face them, I actually look them straight in the eye and remember who and whose I am. My faith has brought me to and through some rough patches for which I remain grateful. We have to be willing to exercise our resilience muscles to get to the joy we seek that comes with living life on our own terms and unapologetically. Have you ever felt that dream brewing in your belly but popped a Tums in your mouth to quiet it down because you were afraid to let it rumble too loud? Have you ever wished for something half-heartedly because to wish for it fully might mean some folks would be uncomfortable with your passion in your pursuit of that dream?

I'm here to remind you to push past fear. It was doing this that allowed me to go back to school at 50 years old to pursue my master's degree to become a Licensed Marriage Family Therapist. That push led me to pursue a post graduate certificate degree in The Psychology of Trauma to better my work with survivors of sexual assault, human sex-trafficking, and postwar veterans. That push allowed me to begin my doctorate degree four months before my 60ᵗʰ birthday, when many of my peers are planning for retirement. That same push drives me every day to live life fuller than the day before. I know there are times when that push gets interrupted by doubt, fear, and negative self-talk, but I take a deep breath and say NO! I take a deeper breath and say absolutely NOT. I take yet a deeper breath still and remember who I am, where I come from, and reset my GPS to look forward toward where I'm going.

I encourage you all to do the same…Push. There will be times when you may not feel you can accomplish any task set before you. In those times, you must reach farther, dig deeper, and push harder. Do not lose sight of your dream. You may sometimes need to shift your course but never get off track. There will be stumbling blocks along the way - use them as the bricks to build the foundation for your success. Step into your Who-You-Are-Ness, and remember, "When life gives you lemons, don't just make lemonade…You gotta suck on them till they taste like chocolate." Live loved y'all!

About Shawn LaRe' Brinkley

Shawn LaRé Brinkley is a positive energetic spirit, most often described as a "people" person. Professionally, Mrs. Brinkley is a Licensed Marriage Family Therapist, in private practice; Living Loved Pathways to Holistic Healing. Additionally, she is a Certified Trauma Recovery Specialist, Transformation Coach, Mindfulness Practitioner, Certified Laughter Yoga Instructor and Speaker/Presenter/Trainer. Currently Shawn LaRe' is working on her Doctorate in General Psychology, with an emphasis in Performance Psychology, as she considers herself a lifelong learner as well as a teacher of her acquired life lessons. She lives life to the fullest and believes love, laughter, and ADHD are her superpowers. Her philosophy is, "When life gives you lemons, you must not just make lemonade, you must suck on them til' they taste like chocolate. Brinkley credits her tenacious spirit to her mantra by which she lives "every set back is a comeback waiting for you to come to it."

SHEILA FARR

Finding Your Voice
Sheila Farr

"Do you have the courage to bring forth the treasures that are hidden within you?" ~ Jack Gilbert

The world is filled with voices that will tell you that you can't. Like many women, I spent years listening to the voices of discouragement, limitations, and misguided focus. However, not long ago, I began listening to the voices from my past that vigorously pushed me forward. I stepped out from behind the curtain of doubt and fear and began cutting a new path through unfamiliar territory; and life, for me, became incredibly exciting!

As a college freshman on my first day of orientation, my advisor took one look at my SAT scores and told me I'd be lucky to graduate from any college, much less the prestigious Wesleyan college where I'd just enrolled. What he didn't know is just a short four months earlier, my only plan for my future was to excel at typing and shorthand, so I would be prepared to compete for a secretarial position at a local air force base: I had absolutely no intention of attending college. I had the dream, but because I came from a working-class family and hadn't really saved to attend college, my family and I prepared for me to enter the workforce full-time directly after high school graduation. Had it not been for the voice of an incredibly engaging and kind high school typing teacher, I might never have recognized my dream to become a college graduate. She encouraged me to pursue college as an option after graduation and even went as far as to obtain the actual college application for me. My parents were dumb-founded when I walked in with a college application the spring before my graduation, but we said a prayer and as always, my parents found a way to bless me with the gift of a college education.

I have always had a passion for learning and helping others grow. During my first year of college, I started working at a local retail chain, where my first supervisor noticed my desire to help others. He was incredibly encouraging, appreciated my work ethic, and cheered me on as he watched me try to teach and grow my co-workers. He taught me to plan, work hard, and focus on small goals that could help move me closer to achieving my larger goals in life. Even though I wasn't exactly sure where I was going, I knew I was destined to do something *more* - I just wasn't sure what my more was! When I was 26, I joined the U.S. Air Force Reserve and it was in basic training I experienced my first *real* accomplishment: being an honor graduate of Basic Military Training (BMT). It might sound like a small thing, but for a country girl from Warner Robins, Georgia, with no real direction for her life, it was huge!

After I graduated BMT, I worked as a personnel specialist for the Department of Defense. It was both my civilian job and my job in the military. I had a female supervisor in my civilian job who taught me the importance of self-promotion and stepping up into roles with higher responsibility. Because our jobs were competitive, with both men and women competing for higher-paying jobs, she stressed the importance of broadening my education and gaining additional certifications in specialized areas of expertise. Her voice of support and elevation would set me apart from others and could propel me forward into opportunities I might not otherwise have. During this time, I was still struggling to complete my degree, but I was making progress by continuing to take classes and work full-time. I was continuously working to push forward.

As I moved around with my military position, I landed a job in the medical field. This job led me to a supervisor who was obsessed with power and taught me all I did *not* want to be if I were to ever come into a position of leadership. Hers was a voice of discouragement, preventing me from learning on the job, trying to keep me in a box of containment, limiting me constantly, and punishing me for the positive influence and encouragement I gave to our staff. Still, I managed to have new learning experiences and gained several new certifications and skills. Even though I didn't try to challenge her or her authority, I could see she didn't like me and was uncomfortable with the informal leadership role our staff automatically bestowed upon me at our clinic. I finally completed my degree and left that position, however, I always remembered the voice of negativity and containment, and prayed I would never lead in that manner when it was my turn to lead others.

My next position in life led me to a place where I had the opportunity to sit across the table from the very student advisor who, when I was 18 years old, told me I would never be a college graduate. Now with both a bachelor's and a master's degree behind me, I worked in the Academic Dean's office where I read applications for tenure and forwarded applications for approval and hire. I had to giggle the day this certain professor's tenure package came across my desk, and I must be honest when I say for a split second I actually considered not pushing it forward for approval. I eventually *did* submit it for approval, but somehow it gave me great satisfaction knowing he was completely wrong and that, when faced with the option of either allowing him to move forward or hold him back to give him a taste of his own nasty medicine, I listened to the voices inside me that reminded me to always strive to do the right thing, regardless of what had been done to me in the past.

Several years later, I moved to the beautiful Mississippi Gulf Coast, where I became the Practice Administrator for a small, privately-owned medical practice. Each year I was there, we grew the practice by a revenue stream until it caught the attention of a larger, corporate practice. By this time, I had started to reflect on the lessons I'd learned from all the voices in my professional past and drew out those pearls of wisdom that could help me continue to grow and I started to share that information with others. I worked hard to put together one of the most dynamic and talented teams I've ever seen. Everyone worked hard toward being the best of the best and I was incredibly proud to be the leader of that vibrant team. Our small practice was sold in the big, impersonal corporate world and it was about that time I heard the voice of the Divine Spirit calling me to step out from a supporting role and into one where I could independently lead; calling me into a roll where I could forge ahead to do something new and bold; calling me to put forth the same level of effort and make the same level of sacrifices for myself and my life that I had – for years – given to ensure the success of others. With that came the start-up of my own small business, Gulf Coast Education and Training, LLC. With personalized training, we focus on the specific needs and challenges of professionals and small businesses and provide them with powerful, practical tools for them to use in the workplace and make a difference. We provide an innovative and interactive learning experience that helps keep our clients engaged and excited! We're the nurturing voice of encouragement to those who pass through our halls.

To be successful in life and in business, I've learned five things that helped me immensely. These are the lessons of the positive voices in my professional life. I teach these to my clients, students, and friends who come to me for career and life advice. This is what I share with them:

1. Know who you are and what you want
2. Develop a plan
3. Put in the work
4. Expect the unexpected – things will always happen that may upset your plan. You need to be able to work through
5. Assess, celebrate, adjust and move forward

My message to those who feel stuck and are in the pit of disappointment regarding the way their life or career looks is to be bold! Listen to those voices that move you forward; get closer to achieving your goals, realizing your dreams, and living the life that brings you the most happiness, fulfillment and joy. Listen to the voices that encourage you – be courageous and step out in faith - and then make your move! There are treasures inside you and someone needs to hear *your* voice!

About Sheila Farr

Sheila Farr, an eternal optimist, is the owner of Gulf Coast Training & Education Services, LLC. She is a teacher, a business leader, an author, and a cheerleader for all who seek to make their dreams come true! At GCTES, Sheila teaches and mentors business professionals, assists them in consistently reaching their career goals and helps them build dynamic teams. A former U.S. Air Force Reserve Personnel Specialist with more than 25 years of human resources and medical administration experience, she is SHRM-certified and holds an M.Ed. from the University of Georgia.

Her message is simple: have a plan and be bold! Step out in faith and gain strength from the voices that move you forward in life. Our Lord did not design us to play small, so when it's your time to shine, step into the light! The world needs the treasures that you hold inside of you!

TANISE MCINNIS

Labeled for Perfection

Tanise McInnis

Can labels define us and keep us trapped in a state of emotional captivity? For some, including myself, yes. I was born into this world a preemie, weighing only 2 pounds, 11 ounces. At a young age I was told that I was a fighter, destined to be in this world. I would need a fighting spirit to endure being homeless, raped, abandoned, and emotionally abused. With these harsh labels, you would think that "the label" you obtain during a traumatic life event is who you would become.

God has a way of taking dreadful situations and using them to catapult you, develop you, and enlarge your territory, ultimately helping you to become who you're meant to be in this life. The road to becoming a servant of others began before I was born. My grandmother endured years of physical and emotional abuse until she escaped to Chicago, IL, raising five children alone. As a little girl, I admired her tenacity and the compassion she showed towards others despite what she had experienced.

How often do we stop to assess our environments and look at who may need help? While in the second grade, having endured several years of emotional abuse, it was a teacher who looked into my eyes and realized the quiet, shy student who sat in her room needed help.

It's in our darkest times God shows up and gives us strength. I was seven years old when my relationship with God was forged. He was with me one lonely night while I'd awakened to hearing my mother crying in the living room. As I entered the living room, I found my step-father in a drunken stupor holding a knife to my mother's neck. I ran back to my room crying and immediately began to pray. I begged him to keep my mother alive and to keep us safe; the essence of feeling safe and protected as a child is vital for growth.

Eventually, it was a lack of well-being, safety and protection that led to homelessness, a secret that I hid. I was ashamed of being homeless for two years, sleeping in an abandoned house, without electricity or water. At times a friend would hide me in her home until her mother left for work. I was able to take a shower as she fixed a slice of toast and hot tea for which I was very grateful. I didn't own a bar of soap, or my own toothbrush. I owned a garbage bag scarce with clothing that, if left for a while, didn't smell so bad anymore. Lord knows I was incapable of washing them. I stopped believing in God! I questioned why He let horrible things happen to me. As much as I tried to turn my back on Him, He never turned His to me. I never knew during this time that my character, appreciation for life or a love for education, empowerment and advocacy were being developed. Like a diamond in the rough, I couldn't see my value. I was too focused on life's traumatic events and the labels that I was carrying around in the same plastic garbage bag my clothes were being kept.

My grandmother always told me, if you can get your education, then no-one can take anything away from you. It was valuable advice that I applied while pursuing my dreams. Despite the given trials while homeless, I was able to enroll in high school, often not eating or having clean clothes. Even through the trials, a sense of belonging was felt in the classroom setting - learning and listening to the teacher gave me a sense of purpose. I strived to earn good grades while believing that a college degree, marriage, or children of my own were out of the question, due to the labels I had. I didn't deserve those nice, normal things (or so I thought). With my faith faltering, I began to question God; and with my overall welfare in jeopardy, I eventually dropped out of high school.

The years afterwards were filled with misguided struggles, and repetitive generational behaviors. I would eventually go on to earn a GED, enrolled in a local community college and landed a volunteer role at a local Department of Family and Children Services. I was exposed to the helping profession of social work and its many facets of practice and met a group of strong-willed, educated, and successful women, who incessantly encouraged me to set goals and further my education at a university. It was during this transition of being encouraged, challenged, and supported that I first began to seek transparency, wholeness and counseling.

Within the first 25 years of my life, similarly to many other women, I had experienced pain, oppression, disenfranchisement, and a host of other factors that can impact one's social, emotional, physical, and mental health. Things began to shift. God placed the right people around me at the right time! We have to be the "right people" for others in need. I was encouraged to seek counseling to deal with the layers of emotional baggage and childhood trauma. It helped in addressing years of emotional scars and provided coping mechanisms. I was now equipped to do something I never imagined. I enrolled in a university and earned a Bachelor's Degree of Social Work, graduating with honors. I continued working within several community-based, low-income, low- socioeconomic grass roots settings, employing efficacy and resourceful case management. As I served in these communities, I found a love for working with children and their families. As my grandmother's words about education rang in my ears, I would further my education and earn a Master's Degree of Social Work. After years of applicable work experience within several diverse settings and obtaining post-graduate clinical supervision, I pursued clinical licensure to become a Licensed Clinical Social Worker as well as a Mississippi State Board-approved Social Work Clinical Supervisor. Afterwards, earning an Educational Specialist Degree in Educational & Counseling Psychology with an emphasis in Mental Health Practices in School Settings and later entering into a Ph.D. program.

I was at the height of my career and accomplishments when after 19 years I was contacted by the local police department informing me that they had discovered the identity of the individual who had broken into my home and raped me. There was a DNA match for a serial rapist. There was finally an identity and he would finally be tried in a court of law. I was about to face one of the most trying times of my life, once again. God had prepared me for this fight, and an internal and external fight it was.

2 Timothy 1:7, "God has not given us the spirit of fear," was the Bible verse that I repeated, as I sat in the court room having to face the individual who had previously taken my voice away and left me with a label. With the love, prayers and support of my family and dearest friends, I faced my

attacker and witnessed his conviction. In that moment, I knew there were no labels, or strongholds that could ever keep me in bondage.

While reading or witnessing someone else's journey, I am often reminded of the times when I didn't feel safe. When I lacked motivation and my primary physiological needs went unmet - shelter, food, rest, and clothing. Self-awareness comes through the process of seeing the impact that unmet needs have on relationships, sense of belonging, self-esteem, friendships and ultimately achieving one's full potential. It's by the grace and will of God that He never left me or let me out of His sight, and He lead me to a profession in which I can serve others. It's been over twenty-three years since the profession of social work entered my life. I sought to begin a career that would provide resources, education, and information to families that are facing trauma, grief and had specialized care needs.

I have had the privilege to do so, by holding a host of supervisory, leadership, grant writing, program manager, mental health clinician positions as well as have enjoyed conducting presentations, trainings and in-services that implement holistic programs that benefit families, communities and school systems.

Everyone has a story, but how one tells their story is depicted through their life lens and visible through the gifts that GOD has blessed them with. The story we tell is forged through trials, successes, actions, pursuits and ultimately sustained by the encouragement, service and support that we give to others, in spite of the pain, odds and the labels that may have caused an impact along the way.

Life experiences helped me to see that labels are not earned by the circumstances that surround you and are within your environment, but rather they are earned by the fight within you. Therefore, I am honored to have some new labels.... mother... survivor... overcomer...business owner... entrepreneur...trailblazer.

About Tanise McInnis

Tanise McInnis is a Licensed Clinical Social Worker with over twenty-three years' experience working in various school-based, community, state and federal agencies employing services to adults, veterans, children, and older adults. Tanise possesses specialized training in working independently to assess the psychosocial functioning of adults and children with emotional, behavioral, social and interpersonal disparities. Her vast and diverse clinical experience has served well within various leadership, supervisory, consultative and mental health therapist roles. She has written grants, facilitated support groups, acted as a community liaison presenting to community agencies. She received her Bachelors & Masters Degrees from the University of Southern Mississippi, an Educational Specialist Degree in Counseling and Educational with an emphasis in Mental Health Practices in Schools from Missouri State University at Columbia, as well as attended Mississippi State University's Educational Leadership Doctoral program. She is the CEO of Empowering Minds Counseling & Consulting Services, LLC, formulated in 2006, established in 2016. Tanise is a wife and mother who is passionate about the special needs population and implementing holistic community-based services.

TANISHA PHILLIPS

From Surviving to Living

Tanisha Phillips

Have you ever head a song that speaks to your life; a song with lyrics that were seemingly written just for you? The past 39 years of my life were depicted in the words of a famous Destiny Child's song, *Survivor:*

> "I'm a survivor, I'm not gon' give up.
> I'm not gon' stop, I'm gon' work harder.
> I'm a survivor. I'm gonna make it.
> I will survive, keep on surviving."

By the age of five, I experienced traumatic events that altered my life. I was sexually assaulted at the hand of a family member, which made life very challenging. This terror ultimately took my voice. Fearing my mother would have taken matters into her own hands, like many survivors I remained quiet and suffered in silence. Consequently, after countless violations I was mentally damaged. By the tender age of seven, I had low self-esteem, anger issues, poor communication skills, and a loss of respect for myself.

I became an unwed teen mother at 18 years old. "Well, your life is going to be very hard," said my mother, but little did she know I was a survivor. I had an "I'm going to make it" mentality. Viewing my son as a blessing allowed me to embrace single parenthood as another obstacle I was given to survive, however, not without cumbersome challenges. It took 14 years to earn my bachelor's degree, which was a major "WIN" for me. Armed with this new sense of confidence, I set my focus on graduate studies; I was not going to give up.

Three months into graduate school, I was hospitalized and diagnosed with congestive heart failure and cardiomyopathy. I remember telling my cardiologist I couldn't stay in the hospital because I didn't have time to be sick (he didn't know this patient was a survivor).

Unfortunately, it wasn't that easy. I had to withdraw from school and change my eating habits and lifestyle. I was not going to stop; I was determined to survive. Perplexed at my outcome, my doctor said, "I've never seen a heart heal itself the way your heart did". I enrolled back in school the next semester.

Needless to say, the last nine months of graduate school tested my faith in becoming a mental health therapist. My son, a senior star basketball player, was involved in an altercation with a gang member at his school. After learning this gang member had recently been released from jail on a gun possession charge, I immediately moved my son and thirteen-year-old daughter to another state. I left my home which I eventually rented, closed my driving school, and commuted 2.5 hours each way to the university three nights a week while completing a 5-hour day internship. While visiting my mother after one of my long commutes, tears fell from my eyes as we held a casual conversation. I didn't know why I was crying, because I wasn't sad. However, my mother reminded me of all the challenges I had recently endured. This is when I realized I was suffering from depression. I had been cruising on autopilot and survival mode for so long I had become detached from my emotions. I sought help from my mental health internship supervisor. This assistance helped me survive graduate school, which led to my successful completion of my master's degree in Mental Health Counseling.

I'm gonna make it. Complete with a mended heart came a newfound love to give back in an unimaginable way. My daughter asked me to adopt a child because she wanted a little brother. My unconditional love for my son and daughter was natural, however, my ability to love someone else's child came into question. After much deliberation, I became a foster mother to a handsome little boy, whom I would adopt five years later.

This journey came with many hurdles and more traumatic experiences. My adopted son came into our home when he was 18 months old, but nine months developmentally delayed. After the discovery of his delay, my daughter and I worked diligently with him and advocated for him.

We went to weekly speech therapy sessions and invested in educational devices and games. By three years old, my son could name all the planets of the solar system, explain the intricacies of a black hole, and could perform basic math calculations. He had overcome his developmental delay and we survived it.

The summer when my son turned 4 years old, he and I would endured an unimaginable traumatic experience. I received a call from the Department of Human Services asking if I would take in another 4-year-old boy. Since my son and daughter have a 13-year age difference, I thought it would be great for him to have a playmate his age. I would have never imagined taking this child into my home would bring about felony abuse charges against me, a child advocate and therapist. Nor would I have imagined having my son removed from our home. How was I going to survive this? My foster child slid down a water slide and hit his cheek on the back of another child's head, causing a hematoma. However, the investigator took my son and my foster child out of my home and refused to talk to witnesses or read affidavits from five nurses who were witnesses. Refusing to lose my son, I retained a lawyer and requested a court hearing. The judge immediately granted my son's placement back into our home with his family. This was a huge victory for us and we celebrated as we prepared for pre-K4.

The first few days of pre-K4 were wonderful, but then the phone calls began every day. I was getting reports of my son screaming for hours, hitting other children and running around the tables and out of the classroom. My son had an ADHD diagnosis, however, the medicine only controlled his focus and hyperactivity. He was later diagnosed with autism, which was a hard hit because I didn't know how to help him. Being a mother of an autistic son was extremely draining, lonely, and internally painful. Autism was not like the other obstacles because despite how hard we worked, this obstacle would not go away. This was the realization of a new life for me. The beginning of my spiritual journey *From Surviving to Living*.

Life is a marathon, not a sprint. Sometimes we don't understand the twist and turns, but it's always a part of the journey. I had successfully survived the obstacles that confronted my life. As I look back, all those obstacles helped birth many successes. I became a homeowner at 24 years old, my oldest son graduated from college, my daughter joined the air force, and my second-grade autistic son is currently on a 4.4 math level and a 4.0 reading level, and my Mental Health Group Practice, Building Behaviors Counseling Service business is flourishing.

I constantly change masks as an entrepreneur, mother to three children (one with special needs), and therapist/advocate. However, I'm a survivor and I live while surviving the obstacles that arise on life's journey.

In 2016, I embarked on my spiritual journey. I learned the importance of meditation (connecting with my inner being), mindfulness (being present in the moment), and gratitude (being thankful for everything). These skills have allowed me to experience a way of living I always longed for, but never thought possible. Meditation (which some call prayer) is my way of surrendering to and being led by my spirit. I'm tapping into my inner power that speaks to me through intuition. This helps me to not feel alone when obstacles arise and gives me the ability to understand that "Everything is always working out for me." Mindfulness allows me to focus on the moment I'm in at that present time. An unpleasant moment in a situation does not make the situation a negative one. Being a foster care parent was wonderful except for the moment felony abuse charges were brought against me. That one moment was not my overall experience and should not be given the power to overshadow the pleasant experiences I had with the children I served. Gratitude is where my peace and joy come from, no matter the moment I'm experiencing. Gratitude is powerful, because it brings positive momentum to the moment you're having. One cannot be thankful and mad at the same time.

Once upon a time I lived the "I will survive and keep on surviving" mantra and it had a purpose at the time. However, as a trailblazer who has scaled some mountains, my new mantra is *"I will live and keep on living."* *From Surviving to Living* is about being alive in every moment, especially the unpleasant ones, and connecting to my inner power. Through this I am able to be present in the moment and thankful for my blessings. I am finally living.

About Tanisha Phillips

Equipped with a vision to create an organization built upon the belief that everyone is born with a purpose to fulfill, Tanisha Phillips co-founded Building Behaviors Counseling Services, LLC in 2014. Tanisha currently serves as the Chief Executive Officer while seeing clients as a Licensed Professional Counselor within the organization.

As a mental health therapist with over ten years of experience, Tanisha has worked with children and adults with a range of psychological and behavioral disorders. As a motivational speaker, she has presented at various conferences focused on mental health and her triumphs on raising a son with autism.

Tanisha holds a B.S. in Business Administration from the University of Phoenix and a M.A. in Mental Health Counseling from Southern University.

Tanisha is the proud mother of two sons (Adrian and Amileon) and one daughter (Dalys).

Tanisha believes she is driven by purpose and an intense desire to help others.

TESS TIMS

Me, Myself and Aye!

Learning to become the author of your own novel.
Come hell or high water.

Tess Tims

The greatest distance in all the universe is that between one human mind and another. Only good communication can bridge that gap, but good communication doesn't happen all that often.

So for most of our lives we're totally alone, even when we're surrounded by close friends and family.

That's why being the author of your own novel is so difficult. You must do it all by yourself.

Each chapter of your novel is written by your thoughts, decisions, actions, and reactions. A chapter could easily be one day in your life, or a year. It could be a relationship or a job. So your life novel can easily become a confusing mish-mash.

I know, I've been there. I've written so many very challenging chapters in my own novel it's a wonder I'm here talking to you at all.

But, I have a Bachelor of Science degree and I worked at NASA for many years – so I think very logically. And the only logical way I've discovered to bring your chaotic novel under your own control can be summed up in one word: LOVE.

You must love the heroine of your novel: Yourself. No matter what she's done in the past, what other people think of her, or how many times she's let you down.

You must never become a naysayer about yourself. You must always be an enthusiastic cheerleader. Become, not a naysayer, but an *aye*-sayer!

So now, far from being alone, you have become an unbeatable team: Me, myself and Aye!

Here's a good example:

I once made so many uninformed choices that I almost lost my life. But I loved myself even more afterwards.

I often think I've transformed myself into the Ultimate Tess – no need for any further work. Then reality comes up and slaps me right in the face.

In this case it nearly killed me.

Years ago, I'd attended a women's conference and was truly bowled over by the female speakers, the confidence they showed and the way they managed to touch me with their wisdom.

I vowed to myself that one day I would be one of those inspirational speakers, so I set my mind to accomplish that goal. It took a long time, but gradually I transformed myself into a very good thinker, motivator and speaker. Finally, I was invited to speak at that very conference.

What a triumph.

What an accomplishment.

What a crushing disappointment.

As circumstances would have it, I never made it to that conference. I nearly lost my life in the floodwaters as it continued to rise. But then God intervened.

While I was driving to my dream conference, it started to rain. It started to pour. It started to dump water on me like I was driving under Niagara Falls. The freeway was getting covered in water, so I decided to get off the freeway and went to the surface streets.

But the floodwaters were even worse here. The water rose higher and higher around my car.

I thought – well, I should get to higher ground. And I did. I found a gas station on high ground, which had recently locked their doors due to the bad weather. I sat there and waited.

But then I had another thought –wouldn't it be nice if I had better high ground? High ground with say, a ladies room? Maybe a coffee bar? A bit of CNN wouldn't hurt!

So I drove off the safe, high ground and right back into the raging flood to look for more comfy high ground.

Oh. My. God.

The water at some points was splashing up to my windows and was flowing so strongly it sometimes picked my car right up and made it float a few feet.

But I found that comfy high ground in a hotel not too far way.

Now, let me tell you – there's nothing worse on earth than being rewarded for acting on an uninformed idea. And I got my reward. Warm coffee bar. Clean women's room. CNN telling me what a deluge it was. Safe, warm, dry, comfy high-ground.

So naturally, having been rewarded before for being really uninformed, my next truly uninformed thought was I could do this again. And after a couple of hours of sitting in the coffee bar, I thought the rain seemed to be slowing down and I can still make that conference.

So I drove off the high ground again and right back into the flood.

Well God, doesn't let you make too many uninformed decisions before He points out your folly. Uninformed walked right up and slapped me in the face.

My car conked out in the high water. The flood flowed past like an angry river. Then it started filling up my car.

I know if you get caught in a flood, you're supposed to get out of your car – but you do that to reach the high ground. There was no high ground. But my car was filling with water. So I got out and walked around, in the dark, still raining cats and dogs, with running water over my knees in a raging river of floodwater.

This was especially scary for me, because I can't swim. So one tiny misstep could have been the end of me.

I slogged up the road, knocking on the doors of the big 18 wheelers which seemed high enough to stay dry in.

No one was interested in taking me in. I didn't get discouraged; I was determined to survive. Suddenly, a sweet 82-year-old man and his son-in-law invited me into their pick-up truck. This is where I stayed for another 24 hours with no food, water, or a way to use the ladies room. Hours had gone by before the first rescue boat showed up. I had no phone signal so I declined to get on the boat, as their job was to only drop me off on dry land. I said to myself "how will my family find me?"

Hours had gone by with still no food or water, boat #2 showed up and asked if the elder man and I wanted to go to shelter. He declined – he didn't want to leave his truck or his son-in–law, who left hours before to find food.

Now it was nightfall again and I was getting concerned. So I began to pray and ask God, "Lord, I know you sent me two rescue boats and I didn't get in, but I promise you if you send me another boat that will take me to a church shelter, I promise you I will get on that boat."

Within 45 minutes, two young guys on a small boat which wasn't a part of the rescue team, decided to bring 50 of their friends with boats to come help out. They headed directly to the small pick-up truck and asked "Mam, are you ready to go to the church shelter?" I said, oh my gosh, look at God. I was rescued by strangers. I never gave up hope or faith. This was a life-altering experience.

This near-death experience and my series of uninformed decisions shook my confidence so badly I had PTSD afterwards. Until I thought about it with my Aye-Sayer mind.

Yes, I did make a series of uninformed mistakes - uninformed choices are the choices you make based on your own understandings and beliefs at that time. And yes, I did spend a very uncomfortable 48 hours in all and I did nearly die. But, even with all that working against me, because of my own actions I survived.

So my considered conclusion:

I AM AMAZING, EVEN WHEN I'M UNINFORMED!

And so are you. Think of all the uninformed things you've done. Life-changing things. Yet here you are, a survivor, reading. So take a blank piece of paper, cut out an arm and hand shape, then throw it over your shoulder and pat yourself on the back.

It's your job, aye-sayer.

This kind of attitude is the basis for the success of my long-running BeautyPreneur program. I teach hair stylists and salon owners how to succeed in an industry where cosmetologists are the lowest-paid licensed professionals: 80-90% of licensees quit before license renewal and 7 out of 10 new salons fail.

To succeed in this toxic environment they must love themselves first. This builds their self-esteem by leaps and bounds and gives them the self-assurance to bring in the BeautyPreneur average of 100 new clients in 30 days.

However, whether you take my BeautyPreneur program or not, here's something concrete you can take away:

You alone are the author of your own novel.

And your heroine is, quite simply, always amazing.

Can we take a vote on that?

The AYES have it.

Contact Tess at:

tess@tesstimsinstitute.com

Website:www.tesstims.com

About Tess Tims

Tess Tims is an ordinary woman who has accomplished truly extraordinary things. By discovering how to transform herself into a better person and learning how to share that knowledge with people all over the country.

She started out as a single teenage mom on welfare, with no job skills and no hope. At one point she could not even pay a $42 water bill. Then she transformed herself. She put herself through college, earned a Bachelor of Science degree and worked at NASA for many years.

She brought that scientific thinking to the chaotic beauty business and is now one of the Top transformational coaches with a successful empire in that industry. This empire includes a successful beauty salon, rewarding hair restoration services for women suffering from hair loss, chemo, alopeci and medical hair loss.

She also teaches courses to help ordinary women and licensed hair-stylists to become AYE-sayers, through her popular Three C's course and the long-running Beauty-Preneur Program. Tess is also a best-selling author, a very popular life-coach and a sought-after speaker.

Tess Tims has not only transformed her own life for the better but has done so for thousands of women, just like you, all across the country.

Contact Tess at:

tess@teachmetess.com

Website:www.tesstims.com

TONI MOORE, ESQ.

Show Up for Success

Toni Moore, Esq.

Once upon a time, I was a wounded girl who suffered trauma from physical and mental abuse, food disparity, and living in the ghetto where dreams are laughed at and fear is nurtured. However, in tenth grade of high school, I got a chance to escape my traumatic life experiences when I was admitted to the Milton Hershey School. But I didn't want to go.

In less than a year of enrollment, I was kicked out of two student homes. I was an "adultified adolescent" who was bitter, angry, and triggered by people who knew my weak spots. So any time they could set me off I violently responded, which caused issues at school. Although I was an adolescent, somehow I knew I needed to graduate from the Milton Hershey School to achieve the type of success I had never seen or heard before. In effect, I had to master my pieces by shaping my mind to see, speak, and do things differently to become a better version of myself.

Through my efforts of working on myself, I not only graduated from the Milton Hershey, but the University of Pennsylvania and the Temple University School of Law, wherein I attained a Juris Doctorate and a Masters in Law. And while the degrees are impressive, holding me up to ensure I didn't fall apart from the pressures of life was hard. But I refused to lose.

Even after I earned my degrees, got married, and entered into boardrooms, courtrooms, classrooms, and stages to share my brilliance, I was failing myself. You see, I had a secret I didn't want any of my clients, church members, or colleagues to know: I was shamefully hiding my blood-stained hands from self-inflicted wounds. I didn't want anyone to know I fell asleep every night just to speed up time until someone rescued me from my reality. I didn't want anyone to know that on nights I barely slept I woke with tears in my eyes because the life I lived didn't reflect my dreams.

I was disappointed about not living my best life. I hated that my pockets weren't filled with the abundance I thought I would create once I climbed up several rungs of the socioeconomic ladder of success. And my heart was broken because the jobs that promised me money, power and success kept me just over broke.

Year after year, Monday through Friday I wondered if the life I lived was reflective of the full capacity of my possibilities. On Saturdays, I escaped to watching television while taking care of the house, bills, children, and social obligations. And on Sundays, I showed up to church in a spiritual burka (a mask, if you will) covering up so no one with spiritual discernment could see I was living beneath my Godly privileges.

Day in, day out, I asked myself if this was the life I lived. Was life about escaping one hellish experience after the other? Was life about finally fitting in, only to later learn I was never cultivated to sit at tables I aspired to sit at? Even worse, did I waste my time papering myself with degrees only to be relegated to the pink ghetto--the places and spaces that powerful men allowed women to bloom?

By day, I was doing the darn thing as a sought after litigator, teacher, lawyer, and counselor in my hot pink lipstick. But by night, I lived a secret life of self-doubt, shame, hurt from unhealed spiritual wounds and mind valleys that wouldn't move. During this season of my life that lasted almost 20 years, I sat on my potential because I didn't know how to overcome what seemed to be a labyrinth of success.

Thankfully, God does all things well in that He will use anything to help us break through mental strongholds--including our brokenness. Just when I thought life was too much to bear, God allowed a series of unfortunate events to happen that forced me to advocate for myself, my legacy, and my destiny.

The day I hit rock bottom was the day I realized I could have died from a young doctor's negligence when one of my fallopian tubes ruptured from an ectopic pregnancy. Almost 12 months prior to my hospitalization, my mother in law had died, I had two ectopic pregnancies, my son was born, one of my sisters was shot, and one of my law partners tried to validate why I was the hardest-working but lowest-paid associate at his firm.

Unfortunately, I had lived as a doormat for so long in hopes of changing my socioeconomic class that loss, disrespect, and pain didn't faze me. But when I learned I could have died from internal bleeding once I went through three cycles of methotrexate, something within me refused to lose.

I had come so far from the poverty lines and worked hard to letting my light shine that I didn't want to die as a mere shadow of my possibilities. And because of what I went through, I can recognize when others are bleeding from their self-inflicted wounds too. Regardless of the size of their impact, influence, or income, I've found that we hurt ourselves most when we sabotage ourselves. Whether secretly dealing with self-worth issues, the Imposter Syndrome, disruptive family members, or speaking negativity over our possibilities, we have the power to overcome any obstacle that tries to keep us from becoming our true selves.

The same way we hurt ourselves, we can help ourselves. Whether dealing with family, lovers, or church hurt, you have the power to heal yourself. What I know for sure is the same way you can work out your own salvation is the same way you can work out your own success. The following are three things I learned to do to become a better version of myself.

First, you must become intentional about what you want. If you want more, speak what you seek. Many of us absently speak about what we don't want, but the real magic happens when you speak what you hope to see. Similarly, if you want to be more, you must believe more is possible. What I've learned during my life experience is that beliefs become thoughts and thoughts become things that you see.

Second, you must harness your power and show up for success. My religious doctrine teaches that we can work out our own salvation. Accordingly, within each moment of everyday, you must show up for success by making decisions that help you reach your goals. From losing weight to saving money for retirement, it's up to you to do the best you can as often as you can. Similarly, when one job no longer fulfills you, it's up to you to find a new job or create one for yourself. No one can ever give you what God planned and purposed for you to do. Otherwise, we would all be successful. Instead, you must assess your goals, find stakeholders, make room for more, and track your steps to ensure your actions help you achieve your dreams.

Lastly, to show up for success, you must become the S.H.E. of your destiny. For some, SHE could stand for self-empowered, holy executive. For others, SHE could stand for self-help educator. For my church girls, SHE could stand for Someone HE empowers. For others, SHE could stand for side-hustling entrepreneur. And still others, SHE could stand for self-healed evidence that God does all things well. Whatever SHE you need to be, be her no matter what.

Never forget when you show up for success that your gifts make room for you. Just know that nothing in this world can keep you from living the life you deserve and desire BUT you. So instead of watching and waiting for a miracle, work out your own salvation. Instead of speaking negatively over your life, speak what you seek. And more importantly, do whatever it takes to show up for success.

Toni Moore, Esquire, is a highly sought after business law attorney, adjunct professor and Women's Empowerment Speaker who empowers women to own their currency to protect their legacy.

About Toni Moore, Esq.

Toni Moore, Esquire, is an Intellectual Property Attorney and Business Development Strategist with over twenty years of business structuring, real estate, asset protection and estate planning experience. For more than 20 years, Toni has created companies, restructured companies, developed Strategic Plans and assessed Corporate Compliance Plans, Policies and Procedures to help business women uplevel their success. Throughout her professional career, she has worked at financial firms, mid-sized law firms, corporations, colleges, universities and faith-based organizations. As the CEO of the Moore Legal Firm and the Sheleaders Consulting Firm Toni is passionate about empowering her clients to create wealth, build a legacy and design a dream lifestyle through entrepreneurship.

ARLANA HARGRAVE

Learning Me
Arlana Payton Hargrave

"Girl, let me tell you," I began with someone I hadn't seen in many years. "I'm doing well now, but it's not always been this way." I proceeded to tell them my story.

I met my boyfriend in 1988 and we lived together for 5 years before deciding to marry.

Soon after we had our first child but in 1998, ten years after we met and when our first child was just three, my husband was diagnosed with leukemia. This was devastating news because we were both only 28 years old. The doctor told him he had only 5 years to live. We couldn't believe it.

Here we were with a three-year-old and an unborn baby receiving such a dismal diagnosis. My husband decided he was going to fight with everything he had. Little did he know this wouldn't be easy.

He began his chemo treatments and they were taking a toll on him. He was very weak and he couldn't not work. He was so sick he even had to leave as soon as the baby was born a few months later.

His health continued to be up and down and I would give some of his chemo treatments at home because he could have a hard time dealing with injections in the nurses' office. The doctor gave me special permission to inject him at home. Even this was an ordeal because he was terrified of needles.

After a few years of treatment, he went into remission and we were excited. His blood counts were within normal limits and we were able to continue with a normal life. Or so I thought!

His demeanor began to change and he was often mean towards me. He never physically hurt me but he would be very emotionally abusive. I'm not sure what was going on with him. Perhaps he was healing from the trauma. At that time, I felt I couldn't handle the situation any longer.

I decided to file for divorce and we officially separated in 2001. Unfortunately, during that time he became sicker and eventually died in 2003. I was devastated! This was the man I'd had my children with, the man I spent most of my adult life with and been with since we were 17. This man was the only reason I was even living in Natchez, Mississippi. Before I met him, I had only heard of Natchez in history class.

Once the funeral was over and they shoveled the first pile of dirt over the casket, I just felt empty. I was just so miserable. I really don't even remember the funeral at all. All I knew was the love of my life was gone. He was given 5 years to live and he lived just beyond that by 3 months. He was just 33.

A man suddenly appeared to me at the funeral. He held out his hands and he said, "On behalf of the funeral home, we would like to extend our deepest heartfelt sympathy for your loss." I thought it was so sweet. Even though I knew they probably say this several times a day and to many people during a funeral.

This man was medium height he had brown skin and was young and handsome! After he made his speech, he hugged me. I felt something! I'm not sure what it was, but he said if I needed anything or if there was anything they could do, I should call the funeral home.

The funeral was on a Saturday and on the following Monday, I called the funeral home and asked for that young man. I came to find out that he was only 23 years old. I repeated his offer back to him, that if I needed anything I should call. I told him I was calling because this was "personal" and not business.

We began to date shortly after and everything progressed quickly. He was loving, caring, giving, and very mature for a 23–year-old. Everything I needed he gave me. I don't know if, looking back, I was in love, in lust, grieving or all of the above!

We were married after just 5 months of dating and he moved in with me. Shortly after, about a couple of years later, things begin to go downhill. I don't know what triggered it or when it started.

The first time he hit me I was in total shock. The man who taught Sunday school, drove the church van and who helped all the old ladies to their seats, had hit me!

He apologized in words, in the bedroom, with flowers, in any other way he could. I thought... Well okay, he'd made a mistake. But that was only the first time.

There were numerous other times. He would never hit me in the face, because then people would know. We always went to church, out to eat, and other places as a family. Anytime we disagreed on something, there would be a fight.

And there were so many of them! I even had to jump out of the van once because he tried to hurt me in the church van. Another time, I had to leave home and call his mom to pick me up because he was trying to hurt me again. He even tried to hurt me at his mom's house!

He had so many women. I even got into a fight with one of these women at the funeral home. There was a wake going on and the woman was parked in the back. I asked him why she parked there because it's where workers were parked. He told me he would send her to me so I could ask her. The next thing I knew she pushed me and we fought. It took four men to get me off her. He was with her the next day.

I didn't see the signs! Or at least I think I ignored them. My friend sat listening, teary eyed. "I had no idea! I am so sorry!" she said. She asked me why I didn't leave and I told her I had done so, four times! Plus my kids had been to four different schools in one year when I left him. I even went as far as living and working in Missouri.

After the fourth time leaving him, I decided not to go back. I ended up in a domestic violence shelter. I was so embarrassed. Here I was with a master's degree, 33 years old, and I had allowed a 23 year old to dictate my life! I had bruises physically and mentally. What was I thinking? I have no idea!

I had to get myself together. The person you see today is the result of me learning about *me*. I moved back to my hometown and started over. My kids had to go to different schools but I was determined they would graduate from the same schools in the same district.

Once I told everyone what was going on, I had support from my family, friends, and strangers. I had been hiding a secret. It was just so hard to let people know what had been going on with me and my children. We had been in prison. I had to go certain places, wear certain things, and even use certain beauticians.

Learning about myself, I found I'm outgoing and enjoy meeting and being around people. Now, I'm open to speaking to people about domestic violence and signs to look for that shouldn't be ignored. I'm open to sharing my story with anyone. I know there's no reason to be embarrassed. It was not my fault!

Currently, I have the fortune of doing anything I strive to do in my life. I have two happy and healthy children and a beautiful granddaughter. I have been a nurse almost 30 years and I'm the owner of a CPR business. I also work as a nursing supervisor at a behavioral health hospital, and a realtor. I know now there is nothing I cannot do and nobody dictates my life but me - I surround myself with nothing but positivity daily!

Learning about myself took several years but I am thankful for the opportunity to be here to share my story with others who may be in the same predicament. There's nothing wrong with getting help for yourself and your children. There's no reason to be ashamed or embarrassed.

When I finished telling my story to my friend, she just hugged me and began to cry as she shared a similar story. I offered to help her.

About Arlana Hargrave

Arlana Hargrave is a hardworking professional registered nurse, consultant, and entrepreneur who believes that helping and giving to others is the key to success. She will help anyone in any way she can. She has been a nurse for 28 years and brings her compassion and empathy into the real estate world as an ambassador and engagement leader for EXIT Magnolia Coast Realty. She believes the verse "Give and it shall be given unto you, good measure, pressed down, shaken together and running over." Hargrave believes the more you give, the more you will be given and seeks to give in all facets of her life.

www.ingramcontent.com/pod-product-compliance
Lightning Source LLC
Chambersburg PA
CBHW060603210326
41519CB00014B/3558